It Happened Online

Stories and Strategies for Finding Friends and Lovers

It Happened Online

Jon Rubin

Edited by
Peter Gerardo, Cynthia Meyer, and
Marcia Rubin

Cover Graphic Design by
Chris Douglas

Illustrations by
Astrid Dalins

VMC Press

It Happened Online:
Stories and Strategies for Finding Friends and Lovers.

Published by: VM[C] Press is an Imprint and Trademark of
Vitkin Management Company
PO Box 165830
Miami, FL 33116-5830
USA
Email: books@vmcpress.com

ISBN 978-0-9795144-2-5

First Printing: September, 2007
1 2 4 8 3 6 5 10 7 8

Printed in the United States of America and the United Kingdom

This book is dedicated to everyone searching for true love!

It's just a click away!
It's just a kiss away!

Contents

Acknowledgements

Acknowledgements allow authors to thank the many individuals who were essential in the development of their book. An author may cite his parents, children, business associates or even a particular event that inspired them. In my case, this book would not have been possible if I had remained married. I can easily say that dating, despite its ups and downs, is preferable to being unhappily married. I have only one person, other than myself, that who is responsible for my being able to write this book.

I'd also like to thank Debbie and Hope, two dear friends who put up with me during the course of writing this book. The three of us endured the trials and tribulations shared by millions of single people around the world.

I must also thank both my children, Daniel and Sharon, who endured the hardships and survived my dating career. Even though they would probably prefer to remain anonymous (so they would be able to at least retain "plausible deniability" of being related to me), sorry, it's too late for that! Once you read the book, you will most certainly understand at least some of their concerns.

On the other hand, I believe that Marcia's children, Eric and Elliot, would like to thank the author for making their mom happy once again, thus limiting the time she has available to pry into every facet of their lives.

The awesome book cover was designed by Chris Douglas. The clever illustrations were conceived and drawn by Astrid Dalins.

I'd also like to thank my editors Peter Gerardo, Cynthia Meyer, and Marcia Rubin.

Finally, thank you to Marcia, who found me on the Internet. Marcia not only encouraged me to finish this book, but she's the reason this book has a happy epilogue. Marcia, I am still crazy about you...or am I just crazy???? Marcia agreed, though a bit reluctantly, to allow me to include several of her stories in the book.

Due to the nature of this book, there are several trademarks and a few copyright names referenced. They are the trademarks and copyright names that belong to their respective companies.

One more note before we begin. The names of all the individuals mentioned in this book other than Jon, Marcia, my cousin and her husband, have been changed to protect their privacy.

Love doesn't make the world go 'round.
Love is what makes the ride worthwhile.

Franklin P. Jones

00
00

Introduction

Love is a canvas
furnished by nature
and embroidered by imagination.
-Voltaire

Was it too much to ask for when all I required was to find someone that I could love? All I really wanted was to wake up in the middle of the night, glance over at my lover and realize just how deeply in love I was. Was it too much to believe that I should and could find the perfect partner, at least perfect for me? Someone to share life's precious moments together, to live and to love until death do us part? It certainly didn't seem like it would be too difficult a task just a few months after my separation when I first set out on my journey.

However, I quickly realized that I was clueless in the current nuances of dating. Let's face it...I'd been out of the loop for quite a while. In fact, I quickly discovered that I lacked the self confidence required to start dating again. Would anyone even want to go on a date with me??? After nearly 20 years of marriage, how and where was I to begin? How could I possibly start dating again? Even if the very first person I would meet was the perfect match for me, I realized that I would still have to partake in some form of the dating ritual of which I was sorely out of practice.

The first problem I thought of was where was I supposed to meet someone that might actually go out with me? Should I rely on my friends and allow them to become my matchmaker? Should I look for love at the local watering hole or a trendy night spot? Should I begin my search in the produce aisle at my neighborhood grocery store or perhaps I should employ the Dewey Decimal System to find love at my local library? I came to the realization that there existed a multitude of possibilities, all of which I didn't feel particularly comfortable with in my search for love.

Then, one day with my trusty computer at my fingertips, I came across some singles ads on my Internet host's site. I perused them for several weeks and finally got up the nerve to respond to a few of the ads. To my complete amazement, I actually found someone that would go out on a date with me and liked me well enough to hold my hand. WOW! What a boost it was to my self confidence when that first good night kiss occurred. In fact, once that kiss occurred, I knew I was back in the dating saddle (so to speak) again.

After several years of dating and having been through three good, but not great, longer term relationships, it hit me that I did not need to settle for pretty good. I not only wanted a lover, but a best friend who was completely compatible with how I viewed and approached life. I wanted the whole enchilada! So the quest continued.

Looking back on my six years of dating, I realized that other than being set up by my friends for one date and meeting a wonderful lady on a golf course in the middle of a rain storm, everyone I met (all 150 women), I met through the Internet.

In my own humble opinion (IMOHO), Internet Dating is without a doubt the best place to meet the love of your life. Given all the other possible places to meet someone, many of which will be discussed in this book, I believe that your best chance for success is via the Internet. The simple answer is in the numbers. With over 100 million profiles online today, it is only a matter of time and effort for you to meet your soul mate.

Although this guide is designed for anyone interested in Internet Dating, a lot of the content pertains to people who are either divorced/separated or who have endured at least one long-term relationship. I also recognize that when it comes to Internet Dating, some of you over the age of 45 may suffer from two additional handicaps:

1. You may not be as familiar with personal computers and Internet technology as your younger peers, who seem to have acquired their expertise in the womb. Please rest assured that you can easily learn how to navigate the various websites and be successful.

2. You may think there's a stigma (i.e., "loser") attached to people who haven't found that special someone through "conventional" means.

In either case, please realize that you're in good company and there are plenty of you out there. Unless you're a confirmed technophobe, who's decided not to bother with any technology introduced since 1970, learning the basics of Internet Dating is as simple as it is fun. As for any "stigma," there's no such thing, at least as far as I can tell.

By the way, if any of you have tried "computer dating" rest assured that Internet Dating is light years ahead of that. Computer dating services tried to play matchmaker using information provided by their paying members through questionnaires, essays, etc. Unfortunately, members had absolutely no control over the process. One friend who tried computer dating told me that he was guaranteed at least three "matches" per month by his service. Each "match" consisted of a postcard that featured the name and telephone number of his next "date." From that point on, he was on his own. After too many disastrous encounters, my friend wrote the president of the service, demanding his money back. In his letter, he said, "my odds of finding a good match would have been greater if I would have walked blindfolded onto a bus and tapped someone on the shoulder at random." He eventually received his refund.

By contrast, Internet Dating opens the "window" to potential individuals also searching for that special relationship. No other avenue affords such opportunity or control for meeting others as Internet Dating. With just a click of your fingertips on your keyboard, you're in control. It's up to you to decide who you want to contact and to whom you'll respond. It's your choice whether to meet dozens of people every month, just one a week or none at all. In essence, Internet Dating allows you become your own matchmaker!

The Internet provides you with a vehicle that allows you to exert a tremendous amount of power, so be careful how you use it. There are a few simple, but important, guidelines you should follow if you want to emerge triumphant, and not trampled, from your Internet Dating experiences.

Let me say this clearly: do not be afraid to meet someone! Just follow the rules and, most importantly, use your head. If you're going to err, err on the side of safety and caution. I've included some humorous stories to illustrate what can go wrong, but in my experience and those of my friends, almost all online meetings never reach "horror story" status. Well, at least not "danger" status.

FYI: I've gotten into the habit of calling the initial meetings or dates "Interviews." As you enter into this fun, crazy, wonderful world of Internet Dating, you may discover that your application may be rejected multiple times. Do not despair. I estimate that when selecting appropriate candidates, approximately (at least in my case and others that I know) one in five interviews goes well, and approximately one in 15 turns out to be great. That one great interview is what keeps us all coming back for more. Those of you, who, like me, love the Chicago Cubs, will think these odds are pretty darn good. The rest of you may consider the odds less attractive, more like the chances of winning big on a slot machine. Again, it is that potential for happiness that keeps us all coming back.

You may be upset with me for using the term "Interview" to describe the first meeting. At first, I called these "Dates," but to be honest, I have learned that meeting someone for the first time is not really a date. Since I'll call meeting someone whom we know nothing about a "Blind Date," I'll call the first meeting with an online prospect the "Interview Date." Feel free to call it what you will, but I'm sticking to the term "Interview." I will acknowledge, however, that an Interview Date can turn into a real date rather quickly. So if the first "get together" starts off as an interview and ends in a date, "Cha Ching," the slot machine paid off and that's a very good thing!

Basically, there are three ways people hook up with others online:

1. Through an Internet Dating site.

2. Though a chance meeting in a Chat Room.

3. And finally, through an Online Services Member Profile. Though not specifically designed for dating, various online services allow their members to fill out profiles. Other members can then search the member directory based on sex, marital status, geographic location, hobbies, etc. Once they find yours, they will be able to tell whether or not you are currently online. If you are online, then they can contact you via an Instant Message. If you are not online, they will be able to send you an email.

Personally, I do not endorse the last approach. By posting your profile on these services, you essentially invite anyone and everyone to invade your privacy at any hour when you happen to be online. That's not my personal preference, but only you can decide which method appeals the most to you, and which one works best for you.

It's also necessary to understand that your particular circumstances at any given moment determine what you are looking for. While everyone is looking for his or her soul mate, people in different situations approach dating differently. Those who are recently separated have different needs than those who have been divorced for five years. People who have been single all their lives have different needs than those who recently lost their partner. Whatever your particular needs are, I will attempt to address them.

Since the subject of this book revolves around the Internet, I will use common online acronyms or "Chat Lingo" (where appropriate). For example, you've probably heard the term *LOL* (Laughing Out Loud), which is one of the most commonly used acronyms. Like any language, the content and structure is always evolving, and a glossary of common "Chat Lingo" is located in Appendix A.

While there are several stories in this book that some feel should be cataloged under the Internet Dating Horror Stories category, the purpose of these stories is not to scare you off from Internet Dating but to let you know that, at least for me and many others, despite a few "Horror Stories" the ideal person is most likely out there for you. Simply stated, if I can date and find happiness, so can you!

I would also like to take a moment to forewarn you that, although I try to keep a sense of humor about all of this, there are several chapters in this book that contain absolutely no humor and/or wit. Instead, they feature serious information on how to best use the Internet to find your soul mate. These sections are the Chat Room Chapter, the Internet Dating Site Chapter and The How-To Chapter.

I've never dated women from work, I never liked "hunting" in bars, and most of all I do not allow friends to fix me up (anymore), which can only add tension to or totally destroy an otherwise good friendship. So all things considered, I found that the Internet is, without a doubt, the best way for people to meet. Let me show you how and why.

1 Why Meet People Online?

No One Actually Meets Online They Just Exchange Electronic Data

Before we jump into the world of Internet Dating, I believe that it would be prudent for us to first examine the "conventional" alternatives to Internet Dating. They are:

- Blind dates arranged by "friends"
- Meeting someone at work
- Going to bars and clubs
- At Church, Synagogue or other places of worship
- Personal ads in newspapers or magazines
- At the grocery (or any other) store
- Finding Love in your Zip Code
- Finding Love in your Community

The Attraction Factor

It really doesn't matter how you meet, Cupid might as well stay at home, watching the ball game, when the attraction factor registers a big fat zero.

I'll come clean and admit something right up front that may cause some of you to burn this book in protest. Furthermore, some of you may feel that this particular sentiment of mine is very, very shallow, and in and of itself may make me a poor excuse for a human being. However, I would still like to share this, my innermost feelings on personal attraction, with you.

For me, I absolutely, positively must, without out a doubt, feel an instant physical attraction to my potential partner. Physical attraction, also known as chemistry, must exist for any relationship to begin. That is, unless I happen to be seeking a non-loving, friendship-only relationship. Otherwise, unless the "chemistry" exists, there is absolutely no reason to waste either of our time.

I believe that if we are truly honest with ourselves, then 99.999999 percent of the world's population would agree 100 percent with me. For those of you who only require inner beauty to be attracted to your potential lover, what can I say except, that's not how I feel.

Now, let me quickly add for those of you who haven't burned this book yet because you believe that I am not, in fact, a very, very shallow person. When I am with someone and I have had the opportunity to see and experience their inner beauty, then that person becomes even more beautiful in my eyes.

Blind Dates Arranged by "Friends"

In my experience, letting friends fix you up is like playing Russian roulette with five of the revolver's six chambers loaded. Chances are that everyone is going to get seriously injured: you, your date and your friends.

It's not that your friends don't want you to be happy. It's not that they know absolutely nothing about your personal preferences and tastes (though this is often the case). The problem is that few people, especially married ones, are sufficiently acquainted with two singles that are willing to be fixed up. Your friends may relish the idea of playing matchmaker with the only single people they know. However, the odds that the blind date will lead to anything but embarrassment and recriminations are astronomical. Here are several stories that demonstrate the seriousness of this problem: first mine, followed by several that were told to me.

Before I launched my Internet Dating career, I let myself be fixed up by a friend. His wife believed that a particular friend of hers would be the absolute perfect match for yours truly. Now here's where the trouble began. The woman I was fixed up with was a professional woman, financially secure, and passionate about many of the same things in life that I enjoyed. Like me, she loved skiing and everything to do with the ocean. Personally, I like everything to do with the ocean, except drowning.

Well, my friend's wife created this image in my mind that her friend was indeed my soul mate. After capitulating to their matchmaking scheme, she gave my phone number to her friend. Her friend called the following day, and we talked and talked and talked. Needless to say, we immediately hit it off! We spoke on the phone and began emailing each other several times a day. After a few weeks of this verbal and written repartee, we decided it was time to meet in person. I suggested drinks, dinner and going out afterwards.

Right before I left the house to meet my soul mate, I decided that I'd better not leave anything to chance. So I showered for the second time that day and applied a large quantity of deodorant, just in case we went out dancing later in the evening. Now, what to wear? Having received quite a bit of unsolicited fashion consultation in the days proceeding the date from too many of my female friends, I selected my fashion ensemble, which consisted of a pair of pants and a shirt. On my way to meet her, I stopped by the supermarket and picked out a beautiful bouquet of flowers. Next, I called her on her cell phone, and we described what we were wearing so we would recognize each other at the restaurant's bar. Additionally, she said she was going to be right on-time.

Even though I took an extra shower and stopped for flowers, I arrived early. To say that I was just a little anxious may be an understatement. After all, I was on my way to meet the woman of my dreams, the love of my life, the one with whom I would spend the rest of my days, until death do us part. Thank goodness I layered on that extra deodorant.

I made my way over to the bar and grabbed two stools. I figured that a drink might calm me down a bit, so I ordered a glass of Shiraz wine while waiting. I positioned myself on the stool so that I would be facing the bar's entrance and waited for her to appear. Suddenly, I started hearing my mother's voice in my head, commanding me to sit up straight because slouching would make a terrible first impression...and you know you only have one opportunity to make a first impression. Her not so little voice went on to say that she would not be happy if someone were to judge her parental skills based on a display of bad manners.

Then without too much fanfare, well actually none at all, the woman I was to marry and spend the rest of my natural life with entered the bar. Instantly, I found myself thinking, *OMG* (Oh My God)! I've already confessed to you that I need at least some physical attraction, but there wasn't even a smidgen, none, zero, zilch, nothing!! How did I end up in this situation? How was this possible? We were perfect for each other and had so many things in common. Let me take a moment to clarify an important point. Beauty is indeed in the eyes of the beholder and while I am certain that others would have found her attractive, for me the existence of even a smidgen of physical chemistry was non-existent.

As my mother taught me, I was the perfect gentleman, cordial and considerate while always trying to make the best out of this very bad situation. To say I was disappointed would have been an understatement. On top of everything else, she chewed her food with her mouth open. Doesn't she have her mother in her head telling her how to conduct her life? Maybe my mother could just jump out of my head and into hers to tell her how to eat. We were in a nice Italian restaurant with white linens. Every time she opened her mouth to say something, the Marinara sauce was spritzing absolutely everywhere. I could have used a bit more sauce by that point and I'm not referring to the Marinara sauce. I had more than enough of that all over me!

I began to wonder, with her manners, or lack thereof, just how the heck she managed to maintain a successful professional life. I had to assume that she never had a successful interview or client meeting over a meal, especially one that included spaghetti. Anyway, while time seemed to pass very, very, very slowly, the dinner finally came to an end. However, since I didn't at the time understand the rules of blind dating, meaning you should only meet for a single drink or a cup of coffee, the date continued. It was at that point that I realized that I may not actually require the ocean; if I tried really hard I might be able to drown myself in my still full glass of water!

Since I am always nice, many of the women whom I have met and have not wanted to pursue a relationship with have mistakenly felt that I was interested in them. That particular fault of mine (although some may say it's not a fault) makes saying "don't call me, I'll call you" at the end of the meeting very awkward. Once at the end of a date, a fairly muscular woman whom I had no interest in, grabbed me and planted a kiss on my mouth. *TG* (Thank God) I kept my mouth tightly shut. Man, did I feel violated!

Well, the epilogue to this particular fiasco was that my friend became upset with me. I was upset with him because a guy should always be watching out for another guy. His wife was upset with him over the fact that I didn't like her friend. I never told her what I really thought.

Alas, one can always find new friends, but what about the others who may want to set you up? If you let your parents hook you up, you can't replace them. You will never hear the end of it: "If you only would have listened to me when I introduced you to (*fill in the blank*) ________________!" "He/she (circle correct gender reference) is such a nice and (*fill in the blank*) ___________ boy/girl (circle correct gender reference) that if only you had been (*fill in the blank*) __________________!" "He/she (circle correct gender reference) came from a good, respectable family (optional) and (*fill in the blank*) __________________!" "We had to find new friends because you did not think that (*fill in the blanks*) _______ _________ _________________!"

Okay, okay, so some of you know people who have found the loves of their lives while on blind dates. I am certain that you know many more people that have had little to no success in the blind date arena. That is, if you even personally know anyone who was brave enough to give it a try. Just in case my own personal blind date story did not convince you, I present to you for you consideration, another *BDHS (*Blind Date Horror Story!) Once again, the names have been changed to protect the innocent.

Let's say that your friends "John" and "Mary" assume that you and "Susan" will be a perfect match, because the four of you are friends, separated by just one degree (John and Mary). This may seem like a reasonable assumption, but there's one major flaw: that one degree of separation can make all the difference in the world. Let me show you exactly how this works, using the following case history.

George was a long-time friend of both Joe and Sara, having met the couple 10 years earlier during college. On the other hand, Janet was a recent "work friend" of Joe's. For whatever reason, Joe and Sara decided that they should fix up George and Janet. They began talking up the idea with them. A classic blind date ensued. Without ever having spoken, it was arranged that George and Janet would meet outside a particular restaurant after work. George arrived at the rendezvous a few minutes early, replaying in his mind the physical description of his date and all of the things they allegedly shared in common. No doubt, Janet was doing the same thing as she approached the restaurant.

When she first laid eyes on him, however, it was obvious that Janet was disappointed by George's appearance. On the other hand, George had no problem with her looks. If Janet had been a cartoon character, the word "No" would have popped up in her right eye and the word "Sale!" would have popped up in her left eye. The remainder of the date was a miserable exercise in futility. Recognizing that Janet felt no attraction to him, George went through the motions of the date. Meanwhile, Janet barely paid any attention to him.

Afterward, Janet's relationship with Joe deteriorated from friendly to merely polite. George diplomatically vented his frustrations to both Joe and Sara, which may be the only reason they remained friends. Janet ended up becoming the scapegoat.

Obviously, the problem here was that Janet was merely Joe's "work friend," someone he didn't know very well outside the office. Although Janet may have described, in the abstract, the kind of man she liked, Joe had no "real world" evidence of the men she actually dated. He did, however, know George's tastes, which explains why George *did* find Janet attractive. Obviously, Janet described the traits of men that appealed to her, but did not stress the importance of their physical appearance. So, despite their potential common interests, there was no instant physical attraction for Janet and thus no interest in George.

In this case, the one degree of separation meant that neither person knew what the other looked like. But that's not the only problem caused by the one degree of separation. Even if photos are exchanged or you've casually encountered your friends' friend earlier, there's no guarantee things will go any better. That's because people make friends for vastly different reasons than when they are seeking a romantic relationship.

Poor George! A few years later, he was subjected to an even more humiliating experience, this time at the hands of his friends Jeff and Nicole.

On paper, everything looked perfect:

- George had briefly met Nicole's friend Gina on several occasions, and found her attractive.

- Gina provided oral confirmation to Nicole that she found George attractive.

- Jeff and Nicole arranged for a "no pressure" double date at a local watering hole.

On the appointed evening, Jeff and Nicole provided a last-minute briefing for George while they waited for Gina. Fifteen minutes passed ... a half-hour ... an hour ...ninety minutes.

When Gina finally made her appearance she was visibly drunk. She plopped down at the table, and announced that she was sorry for her tardiness. She'd just come from having sex with her ex-boyfriend and one thing had led to another and time had gotten away from her. Oh, and did she mention that they were now back together?

I won't bother to describe the rest of the evening. Suffice it to say that Nicole was furious. While apologizing to George, she explained that Gina had been her "wild friend" ever since high school. However, Nicole had mistakenly assumed that Gina had outgrown this kind of childish behavior.

There's that one degree of separation again. If George had known about Gina's past, he might have been more cautious about accepting a blind date, even a double date.

I don't mean to suggest that blind dates NEVER work out. They do..........occasionally.

One of my friends went on a blind date that turned into a six-month relationship. One evening, one of his roommates returned from work, talking about a beautiful woman he'd just met on the subway. They'd struck up a conversation over the book he was reading, and things had gone so well that she'd given him her cell phone number. Unfortunately, the roommate was already involved in a serious relationship, but since he found the woman so interesting and attractive, he suggested that my friend call her instead. Well, to make a long story short, my friend called the woman, introduced himself and then explained his roommate's situation. He told her that his roommate was so intrigued with her that he suggested that maybe they should meet. They talked for a while and she finally agreed to meet him on a "Blind Date." Lo and behold, it worked!

Ironically, this last story is the exception that proves the rule. My friend took a complete shot in the dark, and it paid off. In the years that followed, he accepted numerous fix-ups, and none ever progressed beyond the first date. In other words, he had better luck calling a complete stranger than he did trusting his friends' matchmaking abilities.

In my opinion, whenever you trust an intermediary to determine whether someone is your potential soul mate, you've already made your first fatal mistake.

Meeting Someone at Work

Meeting in the workplace is not at all like it was 50 years ago when it was a commonplace occurrence. There's a lot to be said both for and against dating your boss, your subordinates or your peers at work.

Some of the "pros" include:

- A large "talent pool" from which to draw, unless you work from your home-office.
- The opportunity to interact face-to-face before becoming romantically involved.
- Plenty to talk about on your early dates (at least regarding work-related subjects).
- The opportunity to spend extra time together.

The "cons" often include:

- Company policies that prohibit co-workers from dating.
- Various political and economic implications, especially the threat of sexual harassment suits that may arise, especially when supervisors date their subordinates.
- The opportunity to spend too much time together.
- The awkwardness of continuing to work together after the relationship goes sour.

I've never dated anyone that I met at work. This was primarily due to the fact that I have been self-employed for the majority of my working career. The downside of being self-employed is that a large dating pool of potential mates simply does not exist – unless, of course, I feel like dating myself. One can derive some major benefits by dating oneself, well at least for the male species, simply due to the fact that the cost of dating can be roughly cut in half. However, even though you share everything in common with yourself, it can become very lonely after awhile.

Suffice it to say that while I do not have any experience dating at work, I do have friends who have dated colleagues. This sounds like a good time for another trip into the macabre. So here I present to you another shocking tale, as told by a male friend of mine.

Alan was the controller for an employment agency in New York when Lisa joined the firm as an account executive. Alan was instantly attracted to Lisa. She was just his "type": dark hair, straight teeth, flawless skin and ready to laugh at all his jokes. I have no idea why Lisa was attracted to Alan, maybe it was desperation or low self-esteem? Just kidding! Actually, Lisa found him very charming (at least according to Alan), and liked the fact that he laughed at her jokes, especially when she described the owner of their agency using British terminology such as "Blockhead," "Thick as a Brick," or a "Dolt."

It wasn't long before Alan was spending most afternoons in Lisa's office, his feet up on her desk, sharing gossip about the owner. Interestingly enough, the owner just happened to be romantically involved with the company's president (but that's another story). At least twice a week, Alan and Lisa would go out for lunch and/or have drinks together after work.

When it became obvious that Alan was interested in more than friendship, there was only one obstacle: Lisa worried that he was too much of a "ladies man" or a "wolf." I should mention here that Alan and the firm's owner were the only two men in the office, so it would be easy for someone to reach this conclusion. At least, that's how Alan tried to put Lisa's mind at ease.

Anyway, even though the couple became romantically involved, they kept the relationship a secret from their colleagues. In the end, this turned out not to be very difficult since the relationship lasted a mere two weeks.

Within days after they became involved, Alan suddenly became the "Blockhead," "Thick as a Brick," and the "Dolt." That's because he didn't understand why Lisa was now always upset with him.

Why did Alan spend so much time talking with Jennifer, a colleague? What had he said to Vicki, another colleague? In addition to all that, was he secretly attracted to the receptionist?

"You do think she's attractive, right?"

"I'd have to be dead not to think that ... but I'm dating you."

"But if you weren't with me, you'd be with her, right?"

"She's engaged."

"What if she wasn't engaged?"

Well, you can certainly see where this was heading.

Alan was prepared to deal with the Spanish Inquisition for a few more weeks to benefit from the pleasures of this relationship. However, much to his chagrin, Lisa put an end it to it. Fortunately, the termination was swift, painless and amicable...or so it seemed at the time.

Everything went back to normal, maybe even better than normal. Alan and Lisa became great friends, friends who decided it was high time to stop complaining about the boss, and launch their own employment agency.

What subsequently transpired is the reason that this tale is now a part of this book.

Even though Lisa broke off their relationship, she never completely gave up on the possibility of them getting back together. She, in fact, became jealous when Alan started dating other women. However, Lisa's vanity refused to allow her to admit that she was actually jealous. A few months after launching their business, Lisa began encouraging Alan to date one of their vendors, specifically the insurance agent who'd designed their health insurance plan. Actually, Lisa did more than encourage the relationship: she positively egged him on. She wanted to see him fail. On any given day, she might say something like:

"Have you asked Lauren out yet? Why not? Come on! She's really cute. You two would be great together. I don't mind. You and I are just business partners. Go ahead! Have some fun!"

One day Lauren invited the two of them to attend a networking party, which was to be held on a charter boat that would circle Manhattan. Before boarding, Lisa insisted on having a drink at one of the South Street Seaport's many bars, despite the fact that she was something of a lightweight, at least when it came to drinking. After two quick Martinis, Lisa was feeling no pain. As Alan helped her aboard the boat, Lisa was greeted by Lauren. Lisa immediately became the boisterous matchmaker.

After Alan's face turned red with embarrassment, he apologized to Lauren for his partner's drunken behavior, though this actually turned out be a great ice breaker. By the end of the evening, things went so well between Lauren and Alan that they agreed to have dinner together the following week.

Their dinner date went extremely well and shortly thereafter, Alan and Lauren became a genuine couple. It was at that point that Lisa's jealously could no longer be contained. She lashed out at Lauren by canceling their health insurance policy with her firm, and she refused to talk to Alan for three months. Eventually, she left the partnership, moved across the country and launched her own firm in Los Angeles.

The moral here is that dating your colleagues carries certain risks and rewards, but dating your business partner is like swimming in a pool of Great White sharks with an open wound. It's not a matter of *if* everything will blow up in your face, but *when*.

On the other hand, I know of several people who've had nothing but positive experiences dating co-workers. One of my friends met his future wife on the job!

Of course, they were both fired shortly after management discovered that they were dating. You see, the future wife's department was being downsized, and management believed that when the future husband learned this, he'd become demoralized by the "wrong" done to his beloved. So he was let go, too.

Going to Bars and Clubs

I may not be the most experienced guy when it comes to meeting and dating someone from work, but fortunately (or for that matter, unfortunately) I have plenty of experience when it comes to meeting members of the opposite sex in bars and clubs. I'm sure most of you do, too, so I won't dwell on this particular subject.

I just want to take a moment to remind you of the dangers of "Meeting Under the Influence," otherwise known as MUI. Drinking, as we all know, impairs among other things, our judgment. As a result, there are many, many horror stories as a result of MUI.

I will neither confirm nor deny that any of the following MUI scenarios has happened to yours truly, but here's a short list:

- Waking up the morning after you've been out drinking, thinking you had a nice evening, until you roll over and see someone in your bed that you don't recognize.
- Waking up the morning after you've been out drinking, thinking you had a nice evening, until you open your eyes and do not recognize the room you're lying in.
- Waking up the morning after you've been out drinking, thinking you had a nice evening, until you get a phone call asking if you really had a vasectomy.
- Waking up the morning after you've been out drinking, thinking you had a nice evening, until your friend calls and tells you about how you participated in an exceedingly distasteful make out session for the better part of the evening.
- Waking up the morning after you've been out drinking, thinking you had a nice evening, until ... [insert your own MUI story here].

Those found guilty of MUI should be obligated to perform community service. My motto is: "Friends don't let friends meet drunk!" Here is a thought. When going out for a few drinks with a group of friends, maybe you should consider appointing the designated driver the additional duties and responsibilities of being the designated chaperone.

Let's be honest: bars and clubs provide excellent opportunities for one-night stands that you'll barely remember, and probably wish you didn't, the following morning. However, bars and nightclubs are not the ideal venue for establishing meaningful, long-term relationships, just lots of fun... sometimes. Allow me to bring up one more point. If you are planning a big night of drinking and picking up (or being picked up for that matter) a stranger, remember one word: latex...don't leave home without it.

Places of Worship

I am *not* saying that joining a group at your place of worship is a bad idea or even that it will not work. What I *am* saying is that if you do want to meet and date a fellow congregant, then you'd better make sure that it will work, because:

1. Everyone knows everyone's business.

2. You will be the new pew gossip when you start dating

3. If things don't work out, you will be the newer pew gossip.

4. Depending on how it ends, you may be excommunicated from your Church.

5. As a Catholic, you may need to spend additional time in confession explaining your side of the break-up.

6. As a Jew, you may need to attend more than twice a year, asking for additional atonements.

7. For all other religions, I am sure there is an equivalent mode of penitence that you will be required to submit to.

The good news is that if it does work out, then at least you will know where the wedding bells will be ringing.

Having never dated someone that I met at a place of worship, all I can say is, heaven only knows if this would be a good choice for you.

Personal Ads in Newspapers or Magazines

Taking out personal ads is the low-tech equivalent of Internet Dating. The major difference is that this method is a great deal slower. It takes considerably longer to gather meaningful information about a person with this method than it does online.

While I know this low-tech method sometimes works, I'm reminded of a funny, ROFL (Rolling on the Floor Laughing), LMAO (Laughing My Ass Off) story related to me by a friend regarding her old boyfriend. Well, it was funny to everybody except the old boyfriend. With his luck seemingly running low, he decided that he needed a completely different way to meet women. So one morning while perusing the local newspaper he began scanning the

"Looking for Love" ads. He found one that ostensibly sounded great, and wrote to her.

She responded to his note with her phone number. They enjoyed talking to each other so much that they decided to set up a meeting. A rendezvous at a local bar was scheduled for Friday after work. They met and enjoyed a few drinks together. I do hope you were paying attention to the MUI warnings above! After drinks, they moved on to dinner. They danced, kissed and had a great time. In fact, they had such a great time that they decided to see each other the following evening.

The next night, they met at the same place. They drank, had dinner, and danced all night. Then the woman suggested they should find a motel room. He jumped at the chance. To make a long story short, they checked into the motel, jumped into bed, and started fooling around. Fifteen minutes or so into their hot passionate foreplay, my friend's ex-boyfriend decided it was time to slide into third base. To his shock, he discovered his date wasn't a "she," but a "he." Talk about taking a walk on the wild side. He certainly learned his lesson. Let his story serve as another lesson about the dangers of MUI.

Horror stories aside, the biggest drawback to personal ads is the time involved getting to that all-important first meeting. When combined with the fact that only one in five meetings turns out to be worthwhile, the amount of time it takes for you to meet the one good candidate can be ridiculously lengthy. Consider the extremely slow nature of this type of communication. First, you call the paper and place the ad. Depending on how often the publication is printed, you may have to wait up to one week or more until your ad appears. Then, when a prospect is interested in you, they have to write a letter and mail it to the newspaper's classified PO Box. The newspaper then receives their letter(s) and forwards it/them to you, possibly once a week. So by the time you receive your first communication, it is possible that three weeks or more have passed. You write the person back asking for their phone number. Five days later, you receive their number, and finally (two days later), you call them up, only to find out that they went on vacation for two weeks! When you finally meet, spring and summer have passed and now the leaves are turning the fiery orange of fall. You finally enter the rendezvous location, and quickly come to the realization that you wasted half your life to arrive at this moment, only to have the meeting go sour in under a nanosecond (more on this later). In this day and age, this means of communication is akin to taking a stage coach across the country when you could simply hop on a jet.

In addition, unless you can afford to take out several columns in your local newspaper, your ad will be limited to a few short sentences, full of acronyms. For example: SWDPF4SWDM PCCorJ Box 11223. This translates to:

> Single White Divorced Professional Female looking for Single White Divorced Male, Protestant, Catholic, Christian or Jewish. Box 11223 is the newspaper's PO Box that is used to contact the person.

How about this one:

SDJPTKEOWWTDTCLAPOHMSCSOLFS.

This leaves an awful lot open to interpretation, which means that hours' worth of phones calls, emailing and instant messaging may be required to determine whether any given candidate is even worth meeting. And, since personal ads are rarely (if ever) accompanied by photos, you're likely to run into plenty of "no-sale-at-first-sight" encounters. Just in case you were curious as to the interpretation of the previous classified ad. Here it is!

> Single Divorced Jewish Professional Two Kids, Every Other Weekend and Wednesdays, Three Dogs, Two Cats, Low Alimony Payments, Own Home, Movies, Sports, Chinese, Sushi, Opera, Looking for Same

At the Grocery Store

I was once told that the grocery store is a great place to meet a woman. The logic behind this suggestion is that you can encounter and talk to a member of the opposite sex in an innocuous environment where he or she is not expecting to be approached by someone interested in hitting on them. This allows you to be friendly at first, then assuming all goes well, asking if he/she would like to meet you for coffee one day.

Here is the male strategy. You go to a supermarket, and act like the typical male. You enter the store, and begin your search, placing various unneeded items in your basket. Finally, when you locate a potential candidate, you mosey up to her and, looking dazed and confused, ask her for advice about whatever group of items that are located in that particular section of the store. Truth be told, I am a pretty good cook, and I am nearly certain that I know more about cooking then most women, since I watch way too many cooking shows on TV. But, you might consider trying it…who knows, it might work for you.

Here is how it might go:

With a look of despair in your eyes, you turn to an attractive woman and say, "Excuse me. I am recently divorced/separated, and I have no idea how to cook. Is it possible for you to tell me what I need to buy in order to make a meal so I will not shrivel up and die of starvation?"

My friend explained to me that the woman would probably take one look at me and reply, "Oh, you poor fellow. Come with me and I shall feed you and take care of you. On top of that, I will show you all that life has to offer." The two of you stroll through the remaining aisles together, guiding your carts side by side. Occasionally, the carts touch one another. After making small talk and paying for all your unwanted items, you leave the store together and live happily ever after.

As you may have guessed, this never quite happened to me. No matter how pathetic I appeared, and boy, can I look pathetic, it simply didn't work. Well, at least not for me. So, IMOHO (In My Own Humble Opinion), I would skip the grocery store as a viable date-seeking venue. I'll even give you another reason (in the story below) as to why you should avoid hunting for dates in grocery stores, especially the ones where you shop regularly. However, who's to say you won't get lucky? Imagine: you're examining the palatable virtues of an ear of corn when the woman of your dreams approaches, and says, with a look of despair in her eyes, "Excuse me, I am recently divorced/separated and I have no idea..."

Common sense tells me that the reason grocery stores aren't effective dating venues is due to the fact that most people don't visit local supermarkets in search of romance. They're searching for food, soap, plastic wrap and tabloid newspapers, and they certainly don't want to be bothered by a potential "cereal killer."

Likewise, people don't necessarily walk their dogs in order to meet members of the opposite sex (well, at least women don't), but unlike grocery stores, I *do* know men who have found dates this way. The dates never led anywhere. They all went to the dogs, but they were dates, and they involved more than simple conversations surrounding the merits of fresh versus frozen peas. Unfortunately, most of these people ran out of subjects to discuss once they stopped talking about their respective dogs.

Finding Love in Your Zip Code

Let's say you meet someone nearby, be it online or offline. You meet, start dating, become engaged, get married and live happily ever after. Nothing could be better than that!

The problems only occur when the relationship does not end happily ever after. Spontaneity can be great for a relationship – being able to get together at a moment's notice for the three S's, sushi, sake and s--, or anything else. Without a doubt, living near the person you're dating can be fantastic. This is especially true if you lease your car with a low mileage option.

In the previous section, I talked about meeting the love of your life in the grocery store. The real danger of dating local women may actually reside in the grocery store itself. That danger, unbeknownst to you, may be lurking around the corner in aisle number 4. That danger can strike at any moment and without any warning. Let's say that you are at the grocery store and you are picking out the perfect ingredients for a wonderful meal that you are going to cook for your new girlfriend, who just happens to be your new business partner.

Before we go on with this story, we need to travel back in time exactly one year. We arrive at your neighborhood grocery store just as you were scrutinizing an ear of corn.

At that particular moment in time, the woman of your dreams made her way toward you. She is now examining the corn out of the same bin that you are looking through. She turns to you and says, "Excuse me, I am recently divorced and I have no idea how to cook...." So you end up hooking up. You start cooking together, going out to movies and the theater. Simply said, the two of you are having the time of your lives together.

Soon, however, something little goes wrong. This or that begins to happen. In the worse case scenario, this and that happen simultaneously. You start to have disagreements. You are no longer cooking anything together and I'm not talking about roasting turkey. Your relationship turns uglier than husking a stalk of corn only to discover ten thousand maggots having the time of their lives. The relationship comes to a screeching halt: it's ended, over, wrecked, ruined and kaput. The relationship ended on such a sour note that it made lemons look sweet. I sure hope you are getting the picture that I'm painting for you.

Anyway, arriving back to the future, you are in the same grocery store picking out the freshest ingredients in order to cook the most wonderful, delicious, succulent meal ever for your new girlfriend. As you round the dairy section, you pass up the frozen food aisle because you are headed to the fresh food section. Only the freshest produce and meats will do for your new girlfriend. Then, unbeknownst to you, your local ex-girlfriend who still happens to be more than slightly irritated with you, enters the frozen food section and spots you just as you are turning the corner toward the fresh food section. As you move farther into the fresh food section, seemingly out of nowhere, a projectile in the shape of a Turkey is launched over the shelves that separate the frozen poultry from the fresh poultry. BAM (and I am not talking Emeril!), an 18-pound frozen Tom Turkey crashes into your skull, rendering you unconscious.

You wake up dazed and confused, asking if anyone got the license plate of the truck that hit you.

Hopefully you will have learned two valuable lessons from this little morality tale that will allow you to shop safely at your favorite grocery store within your zip code. The first is that you should never go into your grocery store without wearing a helmet. The second, and possibly more important, is that before you date anyone else, you need to ask what may turn out to be the most important question regarding your future health. Do they buy frozen or fresh poultry?

Finding Love in Your Community

Dating within your own community or building provides you with even greater challenges and potentially greater rewards. However, depending on where you live, the following may or may not be an option available to you. You country folk and suburbanites may find that the pickings are mighty slim: that is, unless you live in a condominium complex that attracts a lot of single people, a retirement community or a nursing home with a high percentage of, or soon to be, widows and/or widowers. Other than that, you're likely to be surrounded by plenty of married couples, often with children. So this may or may not be the best source for finding singles, depending on your age and location.

If you live in or near a major city, your odds of meeting eligible people skyrockets, but I still wouldn't play those odds in Vegas, unless you employ online methods to find people in your neighborhood, which strictly speaking, doesn't count as finding neighbors to date in the conventional sense.

No, what I'm referring to is dating thy neighbor that you happen to meet in your building's corridors, lobby, foyer, laundry room, front porch or at the annual neighborhood association's "shindig."

Sure it happens, but you can't count on it.

- How many eligible and interested prospects live on your block or in your building?

- How many opportunities will you have to interact with these prospects, whether by chance or by your own design?

- How willing are you to potentially embarrass and/or alienate your neighbors by "hitting" on them?

- How willing are you to possibly embarrass and/or alienate your neighbors by actually dating them if you should subsequently break up? This is nearly as bad as breaking up with a co-worker.

- Are you willing to move to a particular location on the off chance that you'll find busloads of eligible men or women living there?

If you do manage to connect with a neighbor, the dynamics of dating are similar to dating someone living in the same college dormitory as you do. You get the good and the bad of living in the same building. On the one hand, you're both conveniently located, so arranging dates and the when and where to meet is a breeze. On the other hand, you may find yourself reliving silly and sophomoric scenarios that you'd hoped to seal forever in your high school or college "memories vault." These scenarios include:

- "Was that guy I noticed entering her apartment at midnight her brother, a friend, or another boyfriend?"

- "Should I try to keep my relationship with him a secret, in case it doesn't work out? I don't want the whole building gossiping about us."

- "Should I invite her back to my apartment after the first or second date? I mean, would it be weird if I didn't, since we live in the same building?"

- "Maybe I should break things off before he gets too serious. That way, we can still be good neighbors, and life won't get weird and awkward."

- "God, her place really is a mess. I know she wasn't expecting me over after the first date, but what a dump!"

- "Maybe we shouldn't go out, because if things don't work out, I may have to pick up and move to another zip code."

Remember my friend Alan? Well, about a year before the "Lisa fiasco," he dated a neighbor briefly. On a stifling weekend in mid-summer, Alan was bored out of his mind. All of his friends were either on vacation or otherwise occupied, so the poor, dateless fellow was sitting on the front porch of his Brooklyn brownstone, trying to think of what to do. Along came his upstairs neighbor Susan, an attractive young blond with whom he had exchanged pleasantries a few times, but didn't know very well.

That day they got to talking about the weather and the fact that she was pretty bored as well. It was then that Alan came up with a great, and completely innocent, suggestion. Let's take the subway to Coney Island, check out the beach and maybe try riding the famous Cyclone roller coaster.

He didn't propose this as a romantic date, but within minutes of spreading their towels on the sand at Coney Island, they were making out like high school kids. It's possible that Susan had always had a thing for him, and he'd been too "thick as a brick" to ever notice.

That evening they returned to Alan's apartment, where he prepared dinner, followed by another make-out session on his living room sofa. At some point, however, he apparently went too far in his quest to "round the bases," and Susan excused herself for the night. In fact, she excused herself from the budding relationship. Well, maybe he had gone too far in pressing the physical. Maybe Susan was caught up in "a moment," a very long moment earlier in the day, and then realized that "if things don't work out, I'll have to move to another zip code."

Whatever the case, the next few weeks did become a bit awkward, because Susan never gave Alan an explanation for the sudden withdrawal of her affections and Alan never pressed the issue. After one date, things petered out, so to speak. They exchanged awkward pleasantries for the next year, until Alan decided to move to another zip code.

Conclusion

With the exception of personal ads, the problem with the conventional dating methods mentioned in this chapter is that all of them rely on chance and happenstance. Instead of taking charge of your destiny, you are relying on the chance that:

- You have friends willing and/or able to fix you up on blind dates and that they will still remain your friends, regardless of what transpires.

- You'll meet that special someone at your job, without getting fired.
- You'll meet someone worthwhile in bars, clubs, grocery stores, dog runs, church, synagogue, your apartment building or your dentist's office, and not have to move to another zip code.

I am not saying that these methods won't work or haven't worked for others. I'm just saying it's not likely. Since the Internet has grown, I have heard of only one person who met the love of his life in any of the above ways. I would strongly discourage dating in the workplace, because it is just plain stupid. With the harassment laws the way they are, I would be afraid to ask anyone anything regarding dating, drinks or whatever.

So, for me, I chose and advocate Internet Dating. As a result, I haven't lost any more friends, my relationship with my parents improved, I don't worry about harassment problems at work, and I am in and out of the grocery store in a blink of the eye, with my helmet on, of course!

2 Chat Rooms

No One Actually Chats...
Everyone Just Types

What is a chat room? Simply put, it is a place where people gather electronically. Many of the larger online services offer chat rooms to their members. In addition, several dating websites offer chat rooms, too. A site that offers multiple chat rooms usually gives the rooms various names based on the subject matter.

Chat Room Names

There are two types of chat rooms. One is sanctioned and created by the online service provider, and the other is created by the members themselves. The online service-sanctioned rooms are fairly innocuous, while member-created chat rooms tend to be more risqué.

Typical service-sanctioned rooms have names such as:

- Friends
- Life
- News and Sports
- Romance

Typical member-created chat rooms:

- Hot Tub
- Females Want Men
- Married and Flirting
- NJ over 40

There are even more, um, interesting names that I won't for obvious reasons list here, but I think you get the idea. In addition, some rooms are specifically created for singles of a particular religion, such as "Catholic Singles" or "Jewish Singles," etc. In fact, you can find a chat room to match just about any interest you have.

How do you find these different chat rooms? Usually, the online service offers you a way to search for them. Otherwise, you may have to check with your particular service provider to find out how to navigate to their chat rooms.

Let's say you are ready to find someone to date. You go to the chat room area of an online service and choose an appropriate room. Usually, clicking on a room's name will allow you to enter that room unless it's full. If it's full, don't worry, many services will automatically admit you to a similar room when the one you've requested is full.

When you enter the room, your screen name is added automatically to the list of those already in that room. The list is viewable by all users currently in the room. Depending on the service, you may click or right click on one of those names and see the user's public profile. If that profile is of interest, you may choose to say "hi" to the person, and that's how an online conversation begins.

At this point, you have three choices on how to proceed:

- Type in a message for the whole room to see;
- Send a private message to one user in the room;
- Sit back and wait for someone to send you a message.

A "newbie" (someone new to an online service) will usually be passive and will simply choose option 3. They will read what is being discussed in the room. Then, once they are attuned to the flow of the conversation, provided they like the discussion, they may jump into the conversation.

It's also possible for someone else to read your profile and send you a message that says "hi." You can then look up that person's profile to decide whether you want to respond.

Rules of Engagement

Just as there are rules of etiquette governing face-to-face interactions, there are rules when it comes to Online Chatting. I've developed my own "Rules of Engagement" for Online Chatting.

First, I only respond to those who have posted a publicly viewable profile. A profile will generally contain, at a bare minimum, the following information about a person:

- Location
- Gender
- Marital Status
- Occupation

While the information a user has provided may not always be true, at least it's a starting point. As I said earlier, one should err on the side of safety. In my view, anyone who does not have a complete profile, and is in one of these rooms, has something to hide.

Secondly, I only respond to those who list, at a minimum, their gender, marital status and location. In other words, I'm looking for people who do not have anything to hide and are not afraid to share their information because, like me, they are looking to meet someone and they are upfront about it.

When it comes to online chats, there's also a common lingo. One of the most frequently used acronyms, usually included in a first message, is "a/s/l." This means the sender wants to know your "Age, Sex and Location." If the person initiating the conversation immediately packs her messages with sexual content, I do not respond. This usually indicates to me that they have a number of issues that need to be resolved. I am looking to meet someone for a long-lasting relationship not just a quick "roll in the hay." In fact, I ignore almost anyone who doesn't greet me with a simple "hi," a comment about what is going on in the chat room, or something witty.

Once I begin a chat and realize that this particular person is easy and fun to chat with, I like to be able to see what this person looks like. It's very simple and quick to exchange pictures via email while you are chatting. Some people don't post pictures online, of course. I understand this, especially if they are new to Online Chatting. However, if they are not willing to exchange a picture with me via email, then (again) I feel that they have something to hide or they are simply not ready to date. Uh oh, I am beginning to feel the urge to share several no-picture stories with you…but I'll get to that in a moment.

It's very easy in today's world to get a picture scanned. Most people have a scanner, but if you don't you can usually ask a friend to scan your picture. In the worst case scenario, you can have it done at a local copy shop or computer store, although you will obviously have to pay for it. Of course, with a digital camera and a friend behind it, you can simply upload a picture.

Pictures are a useful part of your communications with another person. Remember, a picture is worth a thousand words, and the person on the other end of the chat would really like to know what you look like. In fact, I think it's so important that I have a lot more to say about exchanging pictures in the next chapter.

My dating rules come about from personal experiences. One of those rules is never, ever meet someone without first viewing his or her picture. This became a "golden" rule after my first experience meeting someone who did not provide a picture. Did I listen to myself? I have to admit that I am being slightly hypocritical when I tell you not to meet anyone without a picture because, for a while, I continued to break that rule. I agreed to meet several women without first seeing their pictures. Each and every time I did this, I wanted to kick myself in the rear because the result was always the same: "No Sale." Just because I was an idiot for not following one of my own golden rules doesn't mean that you have to be an idiot, too.

Here is the reason I caved in and broke the rule the first time. As a newbie, a woman's guarantee that she was attractive was good enough for me. She wrote, "Not only am I attractive, but no guy has ever walked away from me." In reality, a few probably ran, *IMOHO* (In My Own Humble Opinion)! Another woman wrote: "When I'm in the ladies room fixing my makeup, I am the one who the other girls look at with envy" (maybe those were looks of horror, ridicule and/or amusement). So I urge you to take my advice even though I didn't initially. Let me say that I eventually did realize the error of my ways, and I quit meeting women without first seeing their picture.

Whether you exchange photos or not, there is another golden rule you should ALWAYS follow when it comes to online chats. In fact, it's so important that I will repeat it several times throughout this book. **Do not give out your last name, your home or work phone number, where you work, your work address and especially your home address – to anyone. Period!** If you give out your phone number, they can track you down. Many websites allow you to find a street address simply by entering a telephone number.

What if you'd rather chat on the phone instead of online? Well, if someone says that you can call them, at least take the following precautions:

- Use your cell phone.
- Dial *67 before dialing the number. This hides your phone number from the recipient's Caller ID. If their phone has been set to reject

Unknown Callers, then ask them to disable that feature.

If you ignore my advice, and I strongly suggest that you don't, then only give out your cell phone number, which usually can't be traced to a street address. If you do give out your cell phone number, DO NOT leave your last name, place of employment or any other information on your voicemail message that will provide the caller with enough information to locate your home or office.

Lying

One of the first questions that comes to mind whenever you're chatting with someone online is: Are they lying? The dangers of "Digital Repartee" stem from the fact that the Internet allows for anonymity, and people sometimes lie. Personally, I don't believe that the percentage of online falsification is any higher than what takes place in most bars. And in my experience, people tend to lie less online, at least in service-sanctioned, religion-based singles chat rooms.

Personally, I do not understand why people tell outright lies. A bit of embellishment is expected, but I can't understand why people are foolish enough to tell obvious lies that will come back to haunt them later. These lies usually involve, in alphabetical order: age; existence of, and number of, children; height; marital status; photos; sex, and weight. Most people who lie believe (for some odd reason) that once the object of their affection meets them, the lies won't matter. For example, I've met a number of women who have lied about their ages by as much as seven years. I've also met several women who claimed they were divorced but it turned out that they were only separated. In fact, in two cases, they were only mentally separated.

One woman's husband was still living at home and sleeping on the couch. The other husband was sleeping in the kid's tree house, but had to come into the house to use the bathroom and shower. When I heard these and other similar stories, I diligently obeyed that basic gut instinct...RUN!!!! Others have sent pictures depicting themselves six dress sizes smaller than they actually turned out to be. The worst offender will send you a picture of someone else or in one case that I know of, the person scanned a picture out of a magazine.

A Female Friend Recounted the Following Story

One of my friends began conversing with a guy in a singles chat room. They exchanged pictures, chatted online a bit more and then talked by phone. They seemed to like each other, so they set up an Initial Interview. She arrived on time at the restaurant's bar where they were going to meet. It was mid-afternoon, so there was only one other person in the bar. My friend realized, simply by looking at his back, that this man could not be the person she was supposed to meet. She sat at a table and waited for her date to arrive. She ordered a drink and waited for 20 minutes. They had each other's cell phone numbers, so she figured that he would call if there was a problem. She decided to wait another 10 minutes and when he didn't call or show up, she decided to leave. She paid her tab, put on her jacket, and proceeded to head to the door.

As she approached the exit, the man at the bar called out, "Where are you going?" She took one look at this overweight, balding, unattractive older man, and thought "It's none of his business." She turned around, and continued toward the exit. Then he called out her name. She turned around to face him with a look of disdain. He said that he was the person she was supposed to meet. She was furious at the lies this man perpetuated throughout the previous two weeks. He said he scanned the picture he'd sent from a magazine, and since they had developed such a great phone rapport, why should his age and looks matter? My friend said something to him that I can only leave to your imagination, and walked out. She never heard from him again.

While people do lie from time to time, and certainly embellish the facts, the level of deception rarely reaches this magnitude. Normally, someone will simply send you a picture taken years earlier. So, if you receive a photo of someone wearing bell-bottoms and a paisley shirt, or of someone who looks like a fashion model, think twice or ask a few more questions before agreeing to meet.

Online Harassment

There might be an occasion where an individual in whom you have no interest repeatedly continues to email you. This problem is usually easy to fix. Most services allow you to block emails and instant messages sent from a particular member or email address. Some services will reject email sent to you from an address you want blocked so they never even show up in your mailbox. In addition, you always have the option of deleting mail before ever reading it. If you're having a problem with someone and you're unable to stop the instant messages or the emails, contact your service provider and alert them to the problem. There are some very tough laws regarding online harassment, and they exist for your protection.

OCOCD

Obsessive Compulsive Online Chatting Disorder, or *OCOCD* for short, can take over your life. Make no mistake about it: this is a real problem. If you lose the ability to control your urges to chat, the consequences can be devastating. Like any compulsive behavior, such as gambling or drug addiction, OCOCD could cause you to lose your:

- Job
- Friends
- Family

OCOCD is most likely to strike during your first foray into the world of online chat room participation. Given the number of computers now connected to the Internet, it's extremely easy to access chat rooms. That makes it harder and harder for us to resist the Temptations of Chat.

Once a relationship ends, even a terrible one that has been bad for a number of years, the individuals involved in the breakup often feel empty and alone. Since socialization is, like eating, one of the basic requirements of human existence, the lack of human contact can lead to depression and/or other problems. Based on my experience and those of others, the fear of being alone often leads people down one of three socialization paths. In no particular order, they are:

- The person becomes reclusive.
- The person gets extremely caught up with friends and/or family.
- The person becomes a Chataholic.

I'm not a trained psychologist (I haven't even played one on TV), so I can't speak to the dangers of becoming reclusive or ignoring reality and immersing yourself in the lives of those closest to you. However, I do know a thing or two about living the life of a confirmed Chataholic. I have to confess that I am a recovering *OCOCD* addict myself. This occurred very early on, when my social life consisted of meeting someone in person after chatting with her online, or searching online for someone new to meet. Once I established an online repartee with someone, we were always chatting, either online or on the phone.

Every spare moment of my existence revolved around finding a date. I was chatting online, talking on the phone or searching for women online. From the moment I woke up, I was online. I ate lunch in front of the computer. I wrote emails on my laptop while I was riding the train to and from work. If I wasn't emailing, I was talking to someone on the phone. I had dinner in front of the computer. I was on the computer or talking on the phone until I went to bed. My life was devoted to social Internet intercourse. Just to clarify any misinterpretations, I'm only talking about oral and written communications and not something physical!

Luckily, a good friend realized what was going on and gave me a swift kick in the rear. After a grueling intervention by my friends, and after finally facing the realities of my unrelenting need to connect, I was able to overcome my *OCOCD* addiction. I suppose that I was one of the lucky ones, since I really don't have an addictive personality. However, I am still and always will be a recovering Chataholic. If there is not an *OCOCDA* (Obsessive Compulsive Online Chatting Disorder Anonymous) Chapter near you, you may consider forming your own local chapter.

Final Thoughts

Chat rooms can be the ice breaker that you need in your quest to get back into the swing of things. Chat rooms are fun, even if you're not interested in meeting anyone. They can be a nice place to converse and, to a certain extent, live vicariously. My biggest complaint with chat rooms, and the very reason I stopped using them, is the level anonymity of the chat rooms' participants. Without a doubt, anonymity leads to lies and deceit. We will discuss why Internet Dating sites reduce the level of anonymity in the following chapter.

3 Internet Dating Sites

The Promised Land!

Internet Dating sites are the hub of today's dating world! Essentially these sites offer those seeking companionship a venue for posting and perusing personal ads. These are not ads in the sense of a newspaper classified ad. They are, however, a place where men and women looking to be found can post information about themselves, which includes their age, personality traits, and a short biography. In addition, most sites require that the individuals post additional information such as their likes and dislikes, and a description of the type of person and relationship they are searching for. This provides others with an opportunity to narrow their search to help ensure success. I hate to say this, but it's a bit like a meat market – a meat market in cyberspace. But the fundamental and wonderful difference is that through these profiles, you can seek out and qualify individuals who might be just right for you.

When you join a site you fill out a multiple-choice questionnaire about your likes and dislikes. You write a few paragraphs that describe you and what you are looking for in others. In addition, most people upload one or more pictures (hopefully current ones) of themselves.

Once you have joined an Internet Dating site or sites, you are then able to create your profile. Once it has been approved and posted, other members are then able to search for and view your profile. Now that you are a bona fide member, you may also begin your search for potential mates with similar or different traits, but that's up to you. You can then click on an individual's picture or name to read the details about the person that looked interesting to you in your search.

Many, but not all, sites require that you become a subscriber (paying member) in order to initiate contact and/or read email from other subscribers. If you write someone and that person is also a subscriber, he or she will receive your email and have the opportunity to view your profile. If the person believes there's a potential match, he or she will write you back. When people are not interested, however, they should at least be courteous enough to send a *thank you, but no thank you* email.

The problem is: many sites allow you to become a non-paying member with limited rights. As a limited member, you can post your profile and pictures, have your profile viewed by others and receive email. You just won't be able to read the email until you pay the membership fee. The opposite holds true when you are a paying member and you write someone who is not a paying member. The person will not be able to read or respond to your email, and you will never know why the person never responded.

Sites often tease their non-paying members by letting them know, when they sign in, that they have "x" number of emails waiting for them. But alas, you cannot read them unless you are a paying member. It's one of the hooks that the sites use to get non-paying members to pay the membership fee.

As I said before, one of the reasons I prefer an Internet Dating site to a chat room is because it reduces the anonymity. With anonymity reduced, you're less likely to encounter someone who is lying, or worse, someone who is lying about being married and wants to have a little something on the side. So, a dating site in and of itself helps to weed out many of the potential losers you do not want to meet in the first place.

If you are sitting on pins and needles, and just can't wait to get started on an Internet Dating site, skip ahead to Chapter 11. This chapter takes you step-by-step through the entire process, from creating your profile to making your initial contact.

However, if you jump to Chapter 11 now, you will:

1. Miss out on a number of insightful stories that highlight the lowlights of my Internet Dating Career

2. Miss out on plenty of good advice.

BTW (By The Way) my goal is that through your edification of my dating career, you will not be doomed to repeat my failures, and will gain the knowledge needed to achieve a triumphant Internet Dating career.

Setting up a Profile

Once you have made the decision to go online, your first task will be to create and post both your profile and picture(s). In order to create your profile, you will typically have to complete two information gathering sections that will help convey to others who you are and the type of person you are looking for. These sections are:

1. A questionnaire

2. An essay section

The third task will be to upload your picture(s).

Questionnaire

The first portion of the questionnaire will require you to answer some personal questions. Normally, this information is never made available to others. As part of the normal sign-up procedure, you'll probably be presented with the Terms and Conditions of the site, as well as a Privacy Statement. Different sites use different, but similar, terms and conditions. While it's tempting to skip these and simply click the "Accept" button, I cannot recommend highly enough that you take two minutes to read these terms.

Some sites trade information with other sites, and some may sell their mailing lists to those willing to pay for them. Do you really want your personal information shared with other sites? How much junk email do you really want? Read this section carefully, there may be check boxes where you can opt out of their programs to share your information and inform them that you do not wish to receive unsolicited email. If you have any doubts, write the site asking for clarification or simply choose to use a different site.

As I said previously, you're usually asked to provide personal information: your name, address, phone number, etc. This is the information that you never want displayed or sold to anyone. Protect it carefully.

You will then be asked to pick a member name. This is a name that uniquely identifies you and is shown to others as your identifier on the site. You can be creative. In fact, the more people that are on the site, the more creative you need to be. For instance, you could pick something like, "Gr8Woman4U," which others would read as Great Woman for You. Names should be fun and cute, maybe even hinting at an activity or thing that you like. Here are some examples:

- Gr8Guy
- ClassicalGuy
- FitAndTrim
- SportsNut

If you are a female, I would strongly suggest that you avoid the following names:

- GoldDigger
- Easy4All
- KnowSchoolin
- Lookn4Num5
- Whining4U

For guys, I would avoid the following names:

- IAmAPlayer

- Pennyless
- UseYouUp
- CULaterToots

In addition, you will be asked these two critical questions: marital status and birth date. Let me say that honesty really is the best policy. When someone lies here, it's a major turnoff for me. I don't like being misled or lied to. Who does?

Let me be as candid as possible: if you're separated, you will not receive as many initial contacts as you would if you were divorced. I know this is true because I began my assault on the Internet Dating world when I was first separated. Once the divorce was final, I updated my profile from "Separated" to "Divorced," and the number of emails that I received tripled.

The other most fabricated attribute contained in a person's profile is age. This is especially true when someone's birthday causes the decade portion of the age to increase. That is, when the age jumps from 39 to 40, 49 to 50, etc. Most people feel that once they reach this new milestone, a large number of prospects will exclude them from their searches. Many online daters have told me that, in their experiences, people limit their searches to five-year age ranges (for example from 40 to 44). I know this isn't always true. However, I can understand how someone might not want to associate themselves with someone with whom they perceive to be a decade older. All the major services provide members with the flexibility to search down to a specific age. For instance, when I was 47, my preferred dating range was from 44 to 51. I know people lie by as much as seven years. I've even watched as women suddenly became younger! Nowhere else does the Fountain of Youth exist, except on an Internet Dating site!

Many people seem to feel that once someone meets them, the person will no longer care if they were misled or lied to. This may be true in some cases, but not to the majority of people with whom I've spoken.

I've interviewed and dated women between the ages of 34 and 54. Why did I eventually limit myself to searching for women within several years of my age in either direction? Well, first let me say that this wasn't rigid. But, I generally found that women in this age range were most likely to share both my cultural background and have had similar life experiences. In addition, they were often at the same life stage as I was. This meant that for the most part, if they had children, their children were of similar ages to mine. This was very important to me.

Also, it is easier to bond with someone when you grew up with the same music, shared the same issues and (again) have children of similar ages. I'm not saying that these criteria are absolutely necessary, but they tend to increase the odds of finding a good match. Generally, Internet Dating is a numbers game. The more candidates you meet and the more targeted your searches, the greater your chances of finding the perfect match.

I've met women who will say during the Initial Interview, "You know, I have something to tell you." They then go on to say, "I am not exactly divorced" or "I am not exactly 49 years old." Then they would take it personally if *you're* offended, even though they are the ones who lied.

The Biggest "Whopper" Ever?

A "newbie" to the world of Internet Dating, Scott (mid 30's) signed up for an Internet Dating service in hopes of meeting a reasonably attractive woman with a keen interest in the arts, especially music, theater and film. Within 24 hours of posting his profile and photo, he received an email from an interested prospect named Mary. Before responding, he checked out her profile and photo, which revealed a slim brunette who looked to be around 30. Mary claimed that she had a great sense of humor and that she loved comedies, especially American screwball comedies from the '30s and '40s.

For Scott, this seemed like an ideal match, so he didn't waste any time. After exchanging emails over the next few days, they agreed that it was time to meet. She asked that he pick her up at her apartment on Saturday afternoon. From there, they'd grab lunch and catch a matinee.

When the big day arrived, Scott took the subway to Mary's apartment, which turned out not to be an apartment at all but a single-family house. "Maybe she still lives with her parents," he thought, "and was just embarrassed to mention that. What's the worst that could happen?"

Never ask that question!

After he rang the doorbell, the worst DID happen. The woman who answered did not resemble Mary's photograph in the least. She was somewhat overweight, much younger in appearance, and at least according to Scott, looked like she'd let her 10-year-old sister apply her makeup. "Please don't let this be her, please don't let this be her," Scott prayed as he was ushered into the house.

It was her!

Scott was introduced to the entire extended family, including the grandparents, and was then subsequently grilled by the father regarding his background, career and "intentions" for that afternoon. By the time Mary was ready to leave, Scott was desperate to get out of the house.

Over lunch at the local diner, Scott decided to broach the obvious question: why didn't Mary look anything like her photo? At first she seemed confused by the question. After all, it was a recent photo. How could she not look like her own photo? As delicately as possible, Scott described the woman in the photo, and a look of "surprise" swept over Mary's face.

"Oh my God, that's my sister! Oh no, she was supposed to replace her pictures with mine."

According to Mary, her sister had originally signed up for the dating service, but had recently found a great guy, and they were now in a serious relationship. The sister offered Mary the remainder of her paid subscription, and was supposed to have replaced her own photos with Mary's. Ooops. Mary laughed nervously, and even suggested that maybe the mistake wasn't so bad, since people always said the two sisters looked alike. Scott didn't know who those "people" were, but he suspected they were either being very polite or needed glasses.

Scott didn't buy the "mistaken identity" excuse for even a minute. You would have to be completely blind not to notice that the photos on the dating site were not hers. Most likely, Mary deluded herself into believing that she DID look enough like her sister to get away with this "whopper" of a lie. Perhaps she thought that if she posted her own picture she might not have received as many responses.

To her credit and this is the only credit I'll give her, Mary immediately offered to terminate the Interview Date then and there. But at this point, says Scott, they were nearly finished with lunch and he was looking forward to the movie. Scott went through the motions, and then practically ran back to his apartment, kicking himself while simultaneously contemplating how to let everyone on the site know about her.

Let this be a lesson to any of you contemplating big lies. You will be the one that suffers in the end.

Whenever I've discovered that I've been misled regarding marital status, I've terminated the interview immediately. I would prefer someone to be honest and to tell me she is separated, and has a court date scheduled for this or that day, than to mislead me. As far as age is concerned, I have overlooked most instances of lying, but it always bothers me. In one case, it weighed so heavily on me that it became one of the major factors in my decision to discontinue dating the person.

If you are 55 but look 40, there's no reason to lie and claim that you're 49 – you know who you are. If it were me, I'd simply post some flattering photos, mentioning in my profile that the pictures of me are current. There's nothing to be gained by lying. In the end, the truth has a way of always coming out.

If you absolutely, positively feel you need to alter your age so that your profile comes up in certain age-sensitive searches, then at least do the following: please tell the truth in your essay! I have seen women who set their age to be younger for search purposes, but have explained it in their profile, stating their actual age and the reason(s) as to why they lied. This is at least quasi honest.

The next set of questions you will be asked when you sign up are generally straightforward: gender, where you live, religion, hair and eye color (as though the color of one's hair and eyes really matter). These are usually followed by three additional questions that are definitely worthy of further discussion: height, weight and body style.

Again, why would someone lie about these things? Once more, it's probably because the falsifier believes that once the other person meets them, they won't mind having been misled. **WRONG!**

According to the women I know, all men lie about their height. Many women have told me that they almost always deduct two to four inches off what a man claims their height to be. What I really think happens is that when someone catches the same lie twice, they turn this lie into a hard and fast rule. So, if a woman meets two men who are considerably shorter than they claimed on their profile, then that woman will most likely automatically assume that all men lie about their height. By that logic, I should automatically add five to seven years to the age of every woman that I meet. But I didn't do that, and you shouldn't make assumptions like these either.

Speaking of assumptions: *Never assume anything.* I have assumed things, as have others I've met online, and our assumptions are usually dead-on wrong. If you've never heard the old adage about the word "assume," then here it is: "Assuming makes an **ass** out of yo**u** and **me**."

Despite some of what I've written so far, most people are very honest and sincere. Please! Don't let a few liars cause you to give up, especially in the beginning.

Body Type Descriptions

When you fill out your personal information, you will be asked to select your body type from a number of predefined descriptions. Men and women alike can be delusional when it comes to describing themselves. So like a foreign language interpreter, I have tried to interpret how each of these descriptions could be decoded by members of the opposite sex.

Female Body Types

Here is what the typical male believes is the real meaning behind the different body types as described by a female, followed by my interpretation of what (I think) a female believes when she describes her body type. Note:

1. I am not writing what another female thinks about any other female's body type, and

2. 99.9% of all men place initial attraction as the most important aspect of each potential applicant.

Now, don't get mad at me! I am not attempting to be politically correct; I am simply telling you what most men believe.

When a female indicates she is:

- **Average**
    - The male believes she is: Overweight
    - The female believes she is: Average
- **Broad Build**
    - The male believes she is: Overweight with a Big Chest
    - The female believes she is: Broad Build

- **Cuddly**
  - The male believes she is: Very Fat
  - The female believes she is: Cuddly
- **Firm**
  - The male believes she is: Worth Investigating
  - The female believes she is: Firm
- **Firm and Toned**
  - The male believes she is: Worth Investigating
  - The female believes she is: Firm and Toned
- **Lean/thin**
  - The male believes she is: Worth Investigating
  - The female believes she is: Lean/Thin
- **Medium**
  - The male believes she is: Fat
  - The female believes she is: Medium
- **Muscular**
  - The male believes she is: Professional Body Builder
  - The female believes she is: Muscular
- **Petite**
  - The male believes she is: Worth Investigating
  - The female believes she is: Petite

- **Proportional**
  - The male believes she is: Fat
  - The female believes she is: Proportional
- **Rubenesque**
  - The male believes she is: Very Fat
  - The female believes she is: Beautiful
- **Shapely Toned**
  - The male believes she is: Worth Investigating
  - The female believes she is: Shapely Toned
- **Shapely Toned**
  - The male believes she is: Worth Investigating
  - The female believes she is: Shapely Toned
- **Slender**
  - The male believes she is: Worth Investigating
  - The female believes she is: Slender
- **Small frame**
  - The male believes she is: Maybe Worth Investigating
  - The female believes she is: Small frame
- **Soft**
  - The male believes she is: Fat
  - The female believes she is: Soft

- **Toned body**
  - The male believes she is: Worth Investigating
  - The female believes she is: Toned
- **Voluptuous**
  - The male believes she is: Very Fat with Big Breasts
  - The female believes she is: Beautiful
- **Zaftig**
  - The male believes she is: Very, Very Fat
  - The female believes she is: Beautiful

I think that most women are very literal, and describe themselves in the most flattering of terms.

Male Body Types

Here is what the typical male believes when he selects a body type to describe himself, followed by my interpretation of what (I think) a female believes when she views the male's description of his body type. Note: 99.9% of women also say that they need to be physically attracted to their potential applicant.

- **Average**
  - The male believes he is: Perfect
  - The female believes he is: Maybe Worth Investigating

- **Broad build**
    - The male believes he is: Muscular
    - The female believes he is: Fat
- **Cuddly**
    - The male believes he is: Perfect, maybe a bit heavy
    - The female believes he is: Fat
- **Firm & Toned**
    - The male believes he is: Beyond Perfect
    - The female believes he is: Worth Investigating
- **Husky**
    - The male believes he is: Perfect, but a bit heavy
    - The female believes he is: Fat
- **Lean/Thin**
    - The male believes he is: Beyond Perfect
    - The female believes he is: Average
- **Medium**
    - The male believes he is: Perfect
    - The female believes he is: Potential Beer Belly

- **Muscular**
    - The male believes he is: Beyond Perfect
    - The female believes he is: Muscular... Maybe
- **Portly**
    - The male believes he is: Perfect, but a bit heavy
    - The female believes he is: Very Fat
- **Proportioned**
    - The male believes he is: Perfect
    - The female believes he is: Overweight
- **Ripped**
    - The male believes he is: Beyond Perfect
    - The female believes he is: Stoned or drunk
- **Small frame**
    - The male believes he is: Perfect
    - The female believes he is: Wimpy and Skinny
- **Soft**
    - The male believes he is: Perfect, but a bit heavy
    - The female believes he is: Fat

- **Stocky**
  - The male believes he is: Perfect, but a bit heavy
  - The female believes he is: Very Fat
- **Soft and Toned**
  - The male believes he is: Perfect
  - The female believes he is: Fat
- **Toned body**
  - The male believes he is: Beyond Perfect
  - The female believes he is: Worth Investigating

I know that the majority of men describe themselves in the most flattering terms. In the rare case that they are not perfect, men are convinced that a great-looking female prospect that is 20 years younger will be okay with his looks once they actually meet. Who are you kidding, buddy? Join the gym! Note: this may not apply if the man has lots of money, in which case many things can and will be overlooked.

Height/Weight Correlation

Simply stating one's body type does not provide the searcher with enough information to make an informed decision. It's important to correlate someone's height, weight and body type into the decision-making equation. I highly recommend that you post a full body picture with your profile. That way, someone can compare the picture to your height, weight and body description. Armed with that information, the person can determine if you are being truthful (or at least somewhat truthful) regarding your description of your body.

Unfortunately, many people do not state their weight, and just leave it blank. First, let me say that if someone leaves her weight blank, then I will automatically assume the worst. Secondly, I believe that nearly everyone lies about his or her weight. Again, if you are really looking for success and you insist on lying (despite my warnings) regarding your weight, keep it within reason. I would suggest keeping it within five percent of your actual weight. At least, this is somewhat believable.

Essays:
Who You Are and What You Want

When you create an online profile, you're asked to do a bit of writing: about yourself, the person you are looking for, what you like to do on a date, what makes for a good relationship, and so on. The more specific you are, the more likely it is that you'll find someone compatible. Why? Because while some members just look at your picture and decide whether to meet you based solely on looks, most people actually take the time to read your profile and narratives. So it's important to be specific. Even if you have no intention of becoming a member at this time, this is a great exercise to help you better understand yourself and what traits are important to you in a potential mate.

Keep in mind that your profile is an advertisement, one that dozens, if not hundreds, of people will be reading to get a sense of whether they want to buy what you have to sell. I hate to make this process sound like a meat market, but as I said before, it is! Do not rush through the essay section thinking that it's the questionnaire responses and photo that do all the selling. After all, once a potential mate views your photo and decides you might be worth pursuing, what's the next thing that he or she will do? Read your essays!

Also keep in mind that the most desirable candidates may be fielding a hundred emails in the first week after joining the Internet Dating site. My daughter received over 4,500 emails her first year (guess it pays to be 21 and gorgeous!!). To have any hope of besting your competition, your essay must stand out from the crowd. Writing a laundry list of adjectives that describe you probably won't cut the mustard. Maybe you are funny, intelligent, warm, sensitive, independent and caring. But if all you can do is string those vague generalizations together in one sentence, I'd be inclined to think that you're not particularly caring, intelligent or whatever. If you were, you'd have taken the time to write something personal and specific about yourself.

Like the best advertisements, a good essay is neither too long nor too short. A length of 150 to 250 words is ideal. There are also several guidelines for consistently creating advertisements that actually sell the product, which in this case is YOU! Here are a few of them:

- **Target Your Audience.** The first rule of marketing is to tailor your ad to the people most likely to buy your product, or in this case, the people who will be searching for someone like you. Therefore, if you're looking for someone who has a great sense of humor (because like me, you have one too), then inject some humor into your essay. Don't strain your funny bone in the process: you don't want to force the jokes. If you're truly the wit you think you are the humor will flow naturally from your fingertips. On the other hand, if you're into people who like the rugged outdoor life, you might want to write a few sentences about your favorite vacation camping in the backwoods, fishing for trout and hiking to the tops of the tallest mountains.

- **Specifics, Specifics, Specifics.** If you like children, animals and Abraham Lincoln, tell them why. Describe some of your specific thoughts, feelings and/or experiences regarding them. "I love my cats nearly as much as my children, though (fortunately) my children don't drag dead birds into the house on a daily basis." Or, "I'm a real history buff with a keen interest in the Civil War. The first time I visited the battlefield at Gettysburg, I could almost hear the ghosts of the soldiers on Cemetery Ridge." See what I mean? Instead of a laundry list, you've brought your interests, and yourself, to life in the mind of the reader.

- **Keep It Upbeat.** People rarely respond (positively) to anger, depression and moodiness. If you're still getting over your last relationship, if you're depressed, frustrated and lonely, don't vent your anger in the essay section. It's not the proper forum. Instead, wait until:

    - You're ready for the challenge and excitement of a new relationship, and

    - You can inject some positive thoughts and feelings into your writing.

- **Tell the Truth!** I've said it before, I'll say it again and I'll continue to say it later. Tell the truth. Telling lies will destroy any possibility of establishing trust, and your lies will be discovered at some point, especially if you lie about your appearance.

- **Proofread.** Use Spell-check and then manually review your essay for spelling and grammatical errors. Although Spell-check can catch most typos, it can't tell that you wanted to say "you're" and not "your," and it doesn't know that you wanted the word "and" to connect those two phrases, not "an" or "ad." If possible, ask a friend to proofread your essay, too. There's nothing like another pair of eyes to catch any mistakes you've missed. Mistakes sometimes squeak by because you're seeing what you *meant* to write, not what's actually on the screen. After all, I've probably read this book over 20 times and I am certain that both my editors and I have messed won ore too things.

The "About Me" Essay

The first essay that you will need to write is the one that describes who you are. What makes you that desirable, unique individual that someone would be attracted to? This essay is critical, and needs to provide the reader with a genuine glimpse into your personality.

The "About Me" Points

Although you don't want your final essay to read like a laundry list, the best way to get started is to make a list.

- What adjectives best describe me?
- What are some of my more interesting accomplishments?
- What type of restaurants do I like?
- What are some activities that I like to do?

- What are my favorite books, movies, etc.?

To give you an idea of what I am talking about, I have included both Marcia's and my essays for each section.

Here is my own "About Me":

The four words that describe me are: sincere, honest, giving and sensitive. I can also have a playfully wicked sense of humor at times. I have a life that I would like to share with someone, but that person must have a life also, one that includes lots of travel. I ran for political office (state level). I have some acting experience and have even been in a major movie (though most of my role ended up on the cutting-room floor). Let's see, I used to host a radio talk show in Chicago years ago and I still dabble in TV productions. I play the piano (somewhat) and guitar (even less than somewhat). I also have a pilot's license.

As for food, I love sushi with sake, Chinese, Japanese, Italian, Mexican and Thai. I love to cook special meals for the person I care about.

I like the following activities: baseball, boating, rafting, scuba diving, skiing, swimming, tennis, working out and golf.

Here is Marcia's "About Me":

If you enjoy laughter, fun and variety, we should meet. A little about me: my career is challenging and fast paced, which I love, but I truly enjoy the downtime which is possible due to my working hours and a liberal vacation policy. I love the outdoors, and typically walk the dog 2 miles and then bike 4-10 miles daily-great stress reliever in addition to the exercise benefits. I would love to travel more and have experienced a variety of trips including two overseas trips and a one-month road trip out west with my two sons. I am fun, have a great sense of humor and can carry on a conversation with anyone in any situation or environment. I enjoy going out, but can be content at home cooking a nice dinner (another of my many talents!!) and listening to music or watching a movie. I also should mention that I really enjoy sports, especially college football and basketball. My picture is current. I've been told I look younger than my age and that I definitely have a youthful perspective on life.

Next, you will need to describe the person you would like to meet:

The "About You" Essay

The next essay that you will need to write is the one that describes who you are looking for. Describe the person who will make your heart skip a beat when you meet them. Be honest: you should be describing those attributes that are important to you. Articulate both the good attributes that you seek and the negative traits that you want to avoid. Take your cues from past relationships.

The "About You" Points

- What adjectives best describe the person you are looking for?
- What should that person like to do?

- Is there anything special you want or need from that person?
- This is the time to list any of your shallow thoughts. It's better to be upfront instead of having to bring them up later.

Here's my "About You" essay:

I am looking for a normal, intelligent, attractive lady, someone with a head on her shoulders. You should have your life together. You must be independent but love to care for someone and have someone care for you. You are not afraid to express your feelings. You feel comfortable in jeans or formal attire, running through town or vegging out in front of the TV or fireplace. I prefer casual (jeans/shorts) to being dressed up. You should be adventurous and enjoy some of the things that I have listed above. I am also looking for someone to open up new doors for me as well. Unfortunately, for a serious relationship to exist, I must find you physically attractive. Weight should be proportional to height. A supermodel is not what I am looking for.

Marcia's "About You" essay:

Someone comfortable and happy with himself. He should enjoy a variety of activities and usually likes to get up and go (even if it is going somewhere and then sitting and people watching). I am interested in meeting a "truly nice guy" who is active, fun, has a good sense of humor, considerate, knows how to be romantic, full of life and looking to have a good time. Sounds like a lot, but why settle for less!?! I'm not impressed with those who make it their objective to impress or have something to prove. If you can't be yourself with me, please contact someone else.

The "First Date" Essay

The next essay that you will need to write is the one that describes your initial date. My hypothetical first date essay has changed considerably over the past few years. In fact all of your paragraphs can and should evolve over the course of your online dating career. Be simple and honest about how you think a first date should go. Consider adding a bit more of your romantic side – that is, if you have one.

Here's my "The First Date" essay:

First, getting together for a glass of wine or for coffee, then seeing where it goes from there. I love to share a glass of wine in front of the fireplace or at the beach as the sun is setting.

Here's Marcia's "The First Date" essay:

A great conversation that moves from subject to subject without a lull. The discovery of mutual interests plus that spark of "chemistry" and the desire to further investigate the potential.

Do not be afraid to be different. Marcia, my Internet Bride, says that since we live in South Florida, almost every guy writes about romance on the beach as the sun is setting. So according to her, it would stand to reason that if everyone who says they like being romantic at the beach when the sun sets were actually on the beach when the sun was setting, then the beaches would be far too crowed for any romance to occur. Again the simple rule is: Be yourself and try to be unique!

Finally, you want to express exactly what you are really looking for in a relationship. This can take quite a bit of time and thought. Think it through and be honest, because here you can bring up all those life lessons you learned (sometimes the hard way) and what is really important to you.

The "About the Relationship" Essay

Typically, the last type of essay that you will write is about how you feel your relationships should evolve. What is important to you in a relationship? Again, this is a lot like the "About You" essay except instead of describing what you look for in a person, you'll describe what you look for in a relationship.

Here's my "About the Relationship" essay:

> *A soul mate and partner. A person who respects me and whom I respect. We can have similar traits or be opposites, but we must both be willing to communicate with each other. We are better together than apart, since we enrich each other's life. A person who realizes how special I am and who knows how much better life can be when you can share it with someone who loves, respects and appreciates you. Mutual respect is necessary. Honesty, communication and commitment form the basis for a lasting relationship. A good relationship can only be built when each partner is willing to be open and meet the other person half-way.*

Here's Marcia's "About the Relationship" essay:

> *My ideal relationship: Honesty, mutual interests, caring about the other person's feelings, desires, and opinions. Lots of laughs are very important and not taking ourselves too seriously most of the time.*
>
> *My past relationships: That everyone has to be themselves and honest about who they are and what they want in a relationship.*

If you're a good conversationalist, but suffer from writer's block, here's an easy four-step process for writing your essay. I can't promise you'll win the Nobel Prize for literature, but that's not the point, is it?

Step 1: Write a simple bulleted outline that lists, in order, the points you'd like to make about yourself, the kind of person you're looking for, etc. You don't have to bother using Roman numerals and capital letters (like you were taught in high school). Just map out the order in which you'd like to make your points. For example, the bullet list that I used for my "About Me" essay:

- sincere, honest, giving and sensitive
- great sense of humor
- looking for someone like me
- Sushi, Chinese .... Love to cook
- activities

Step 2: Use the outline to help you. Begin by writing short sentences for each of your bullet points. Feel free to refer back to my "About Me" essay to see how I expanded on my bullet points.

If writing is a problem, then consider dictating your essay into a tape recorder. One of the benefits of this approach is that most people think faster than they write, so this step eliminates a lot of time from the writing process. If you do not have a tape recorder, I'll be happy to sell you my mine for the right price. However, the tape has been erased...of course.

Step 3: (Skip to Step 4 if you do not have a tape recorder.) Transcribe your recording, or have it transcribed for you. This is how you put your rough draft into written format.

Step 4: Edit and rewrite your essay, or have someone do it for you. Again, since you're not writing an Oscar-winning screenplay, you don't have to go through 25 different rewrites, although you probably will. Just make sure your essay has a logical flow: that it starts with A and ends with Z. This doesn't require masterful prose. It just takes simple, clear language.

Step 5: If all else fails call upon a close friend that can help you write your essays.

Here's a funny story that was related to me after I completed writing this book. Since I wasn't really sure where the proper location for this story was, I made an executive decision and placed it here for your reading pleasure.

I was visiting my "Aunt" Carol one weekend. (Actually, Aunt is in quotes because she is really my second cousin twice removed, or something like that. I have known and loved her all my life, and have always referred to her as my Aunt.) Anyway, Aunt Carol has a friend, Judy, whose husband passed away several years ago. She was persuaded by her friends that not only should she start dating again, but that Internet Dating was the way to go.

(Editorial note from my Internet Bride: I think it's important to note here that Judy is in her early 70's...you go, Judy!!)

One day Judy came over to visit Aunt Carol while Uncle Ken was not home. They decided to use Ken's home office computer to begin Judy's foray into the world of Internet Dating. They began with the Internet Dating site that was suggested to Judy by several of her friends. The hunt began when they started searching for men in her desired age range.

When they came across a man that seemed promising, they printed out his profile. By the time they finished, they found 10 men that seemed to show at least some promise. Upon seeing that this might be a viable method for meeting potential men to court her, Judy went ahead and signed up for the service. Together they created Judy's profile, and when they were finished, they decided to call it a day. They agreed that they would sign on again the following day to see how many responses there would be to her profile. They turned off the computer and left Ken's office. Inadvertently, they forgot to take the men's profiles that they had printed out.

Well, Uncle Ken showed up about an hour later and went up to his office. He sat down and noticed that there were some printouts in the printer that he did not remember being there when he was in the office earlier in the day. He reached over, picked them up from the tray and began to read. A few minutes later, Ken went in search of Carol with the printouts in hand. When he found her in the kitchen, he held up the stack of men's profiles that were searching for new partners and asked her if there was something she had not told him!

As Carol and I were laughing over this story, Ken walked into the room. He immediately said that he knew that he had nothing to worry about when he found the pictures. However, when I turned my head to look at Carol she stated that indeed he *probably* had nothing to worry about. How is it that women always seem to have the last word????????

Photos

As I said earlier, 99.9% of the world wants to be physically attracted to their mates. For me, photos are a must! According to one Internet Dating site, members who post pictures receive, on average, 10 times the amount of initial contact mail than those who don't post photos.

Many people have told me that when they first start out, they do not want to post their photo. Why not, unless you have something to hide? I know many teachers, doctors and others from all walks of life, who have posted their pictures. I have yet to hear about something bad that's happened as a result of posting a picture on an Internet Dating site. In fact, one evening, while checking out some of the new profiles that were on my favorite Internet Dating site, I came across the profile of my psychologist that I was seeing about my *OCOCD*!

> Confession time... The following week during our session, out of the blue, I turned to her and said. "I'm curious: do you happen to be a Leo?" She asked me how I knew that. I gave her some astrological mumbo jumbo about something or another. She was amazed. Over the next few weeks, I asked her if she had certain hobbies and told her the type of movies and sports I sensed she liked. I finally admitted how I knew this information. We then spent the next

three sessions discussing just how difficult it is to meet someone special.

Not everyone looks exactly like his or her picture in real life, but what's important is that the picture offers a fairly accurate representation of the person. Earlier I discussed the three attributes that were most often misrepresented: the first being marital status, the second being age and the third, a person's appearance. In my opinion, it's important for you to choose a photo of yourself that is slightly above average. I'd rather be surprised when a woman looks better than her picture, than disappointed when she doesn't look as good. You should include at least one picture that shows the entire length of your body.

Searching

When it comes to launching your search for the right person, there's nothing wrong with being specific, unless you're SO specific that you screen out 100% of the members on your dating site.

Okay, so your *ideal* man is 6' 2", weighs 190 pounds, has blue eyes, sandy hair, speaks ancient Greek and owns a yacht (sorry, I'm already taken). Chances are you won't find many men that completely fit the bill. So ask yourself, "Is this the only type of man I'm willing to meet? Am I willing to compromise on any (or all) of those requirements?"

I'm not suggesting you lower your standards or discard your most sacred beliefs. I'm merely recommending that you be honest about who you'd really be willing to meet. For many of us, the ideal woman or man becomes our ideal precisely because they're very hard to find. By all means, feel free to start your search by seeing if that Greek-speaking, yacht-owning gentleman has signed up for the same online service. But if he hasn't (yet), you may want to expand your search criteria.

How many perfect members of the opposite sex are really out there for you to find? I came up with this simple formula that I used. You can use a variation of the formula to determine how many are within your dating range.

1. Take the number of people within a ___ mile radius from where you live. You determine the number of miles that you are willing to travel.
2. Divide it in half to determine the number of men/women in your area.
3. Then multiply that figure by the percentage that are single.
4. Then multiply that figure by the percentage of those men/women who are in your dating age range.
5. (optional) Then multiply that figure by the percentage that shares your religious or spiritual beliefs.
6. Then multiply by the percentage you would be attracted to.
7. Then multiply that figure by the percentage who could be a perfect match for you.

Okay, let's plug some numbers into this formula.

1. 1,000,000 live within a 50 mile radius of me.
2. 500,000 are women (50%).

3. 250,000 are single (50% due to my advanced age).
4. 25,000 of them are within my dating range (10%).
5. (optional) religious choice (not used in this example).
6. 2,500 of them I would find attractive (10%) (See Attraction Percentage Table below).
7. 125 of them could be a perfect match for me (5%).

You can plug in any numbers you feel are right, and enter different variables such as religion if you so desire. The one thing this exercise shows is that there is a pool of potentially perfect matches for you.

The only trouble is how to locate those 125 people. Well, I would venture to say that at least 25% of them are on an Internet Dating site. So that would mean that in my formula there are 31.25 perfect matches available for me on Internet Dating sites.

I've mentioned several times that appearance is critical to most individuals. I've said and will continue to say, that even though you might find me shallow, I absolutely had to be attracted to a woman to be interested in her. Remember, beauty is in the eye of the beholder. Maybe you aren't a movie star, but there is someone out there that will find you attractive. Please see the Attraction Percentage Table on the following page.

Attraction Percentage Table

Rate your looks	Percentage of people that will be attracted to you
10	80%
9	70%
8	60%
7	50%
6	40%
5	30%
4	20%
3	10%
2	5%
1	1%

Geographic Desirability

Due to the Internet's global reach, members of Internet Dating sites usually fall into one of three categories, depending on one member's geographic location vis-à-vis another member's location. Someone can be:

Geographically Desirable - Which is defined as someone who lives within an easy commute from your domicile, where you have the ability to meet each other for dinner or drinks on any given evening.

Geographically Challenged - Just to clear up any misunderstandings, being labeled Geographically Challenged (GC for short) does not mean that this person has no idea which U.S. states border Alaska. Being GC refers to situations in which the location of the two individuals' domiciles makes it difficult to get together for dinner, drinks or anything else at a moment's notice. Getting together for weekends is a definite possibility. The GC couple's travel requirements typically necessitate a one- to three-hour commute each way.

Geographically Undesirable – This is someone who lives so far away that you have to fly to see them or drive in excess of three hours.

The Cost of Dating

While this may be directed more to the men reading this book, there were two main reasons that I chose to date only Geographically Desirable women – ones that lived within an hour's drive of my home. The reasons were simple: time and money. The math is easy. I began my Internet Dating career in earnest in December of 1998. I met Marcia, my Internet Bride, for the first time in July of 2004. During that period of time, I had three relationships (two from the Internet and one resulting from the sharing of an umbrella at a golf course) that lasted just over a year each. In addition, there was one relationship (through the Internet) that lasted for six months. Note: I am not counting the relationship with Marcia, because I ended my dating career the day I met her. (She however didn't end her dating career until at least one month later.) In addition to the previously mentioned relationships, there were probably 10 women whom I dated for approximately six weeks each.

Take the three relationships that lasted one year. Add to that the one relationship that lasted six months, then add to that the 60 weeks or so that I dated various other women. The sum total of months that I was in a relationship added up to 56 months. Subtract the 56 relationship-occupied months from the 78 months that my

Internet Dating career spanned and you end up with my being on the hunt for a total of 22 months. During that 22-month period, I conducted over 150 Interviews. That meant that I had to interview, on average, just over 6.818 women per month. So with 150 interviews resulting in just four relationships lasting six months or longer, the statistical analysis indicated that only 1 in 37.5 Interviews resulted in a longer term relationship, and 1 in 150 caused the wedding bells to ring. So as not to frustrate you with these odds, about 1 in 3 resulted in a pretty good make-out session. Disclaimer: Individual results may vary.

The average cost of each Interview Date was around $50. Each meeting lasted approximately two hours, and required me to drive an hour each way. In the beginning, the costs were higher, because it always included (at a minimum) dinner plus drinks. As I became an Internet Dating veteran, my Interviews consisted only of a couple of drinks and possibly an appetizer. By the time I got to Marcia, the allotted Interview expenditure allowed for a draft beer or a glass of the house wine, plus peanuts or whatever else the bartender was serving up gratis.

So take 150 Interview Dates multiplied by $50 each, and you end up with total of $7,500 plus 600 hours of interviewing and driving time. All that for 136 failed interviews! But I didn't look at it as 136 failed interviews, I viewed it as 50 pretty good make-out sessions and, more importantly, it represented the "means to the end" of finding my bride, Marcia. It was definitely worth every kiss ... I mean every penny and every hour spent to find her!

My point regarding time and money is that, based on your calculations in the previous section, you know that there are definitely a certain number of potentially perfect, Geographically Desirable, candidates for you to meet on the Internet. So, why waste considerably more time and money traveling farther just to find out that the moment you meet each other, it's all wrong? You could just as easily experience the same results at a fraction of the cost and time at a location near you.

Time and money aside, if you are only looking for the occasional relationship that probably won't turn into something more, feel free to skip ahead to "*The Search Begins*" section. On the other hand, if you are looking for a serious relationship, there are several very good reasons why you should limit your search to only those that fall into the Geographically Desirable category, or in the worst case scenario, someone who falls into the Geographically Challenged category.

It is essential to the development of a successful, happy and loving relationship that each of you have time to really get to know the other person. One can only fully acquire such knowledge by spending a significant amount of time with that individual, to see how he or she handles the various situations that life throws their way.

If you only get together every other weekend or (worse) once a month, everyone is always on their best behavior. This is because you are typically so excited to see each other, and hold one another, that all other feelings are set aside. You never quite get a chance to settle down into the day-to-day routine of a relationship. Often, you may only be together for two or three days at a time.

On the positive side of a Geographically Undesirable relationship, you'll never have a date cancelled because of a last-minute meeting. However, on the negative side, you will never be able to get together at a moment's notice for dinner, drinks, to catch the latest movie, or simply an afternoon delight. Spontaneity is completely absent from your relationship, and that's a shame. If one of you has visitation rights with your children, then you probably will choose to spend only the "off" weekends together. Your potential partner never has a chance to see how you interact with your kids, let alone get a chance to meet them. Isn't that critical to the development of a long-term relationship?

If you insist on pursuing a Geographically Undesirable relationship simply because you believe that there does not exist even one compatible person for you within an hour's drive, all I have to say is that you are either:

1. Not trying hard enough to find someone nearby.

2. Creating a situation that will allow you to avoid making a real commitment.

3. Setting yourself up for failure.

That said, there are always exceptions to the rule, and below are the criteria that can allow two Geographically Undesirable people to develop a healthy relationship.

1. If you met someone while you were either in her home town or she was in yours, and

2. Your Interview Date turned into a Real Date, and

3. One of you is not tied down to your current location and is willing to move, and

4. You are willing to spend an extended period of time together, and

NARVESEN

Hotell Continental
Stortingsgata 24/26
0161 Oslo
22-429564
Organisasjonsnr. 983415660 MVA

vittering 1327128

Ant	Navn	Enhetspris	Total/kr
1	MARLBORO MENTHOL 20	80,00	80,00

ubtotal	80,00
VA 25%	16,00
otal	80,00

ottatt
isa 80,00

AX 176602-1
ISA ************8598
tløper:08/2009
5/06/2008 17:12
ef:135844-09220A
peratørnr:4
eløp NOK 80.00

ato:25.06.2008 Tid:17:13:11 Butikknr:804
asse:1 Kasserer: KASSE 1

Narvesen
Har du lyst har du lov

5. The two of you meet nearly all the criteria as described in the "*How to Identify Who is Right for You*" section located near the end of Chapter 4.

If you can answer with a resounding "*Yes*" to each of the five points above, and you can afford the travel expenses, then I say: Go for it!

The Search begins!

People often compare Internet Dating to searching for a job. That's a good analogy. Perhaps it's because I'm self-employed, but I tend to compare Internet Dating to prospecting for new clients. When it comes to reaching prospects, whether they're potential clients for your law firm or potential spouses, depending on one's objective, the majority of people take one of three approaches:

1. The Passive Approach

2. The Mass Marketing Approach

3. The Targeted Approach.

Passive Approach

This is the approach that I took...most of the time. In other words, after I set up my profile, I sat back and waited for women to respond. Again, think what you will, but I believe that the more attractive individuals on Internet Dating sites take this approach. The problem with this approach and the mass marketing approach (described below) is that they reduce the chances for finding the truly right person – that is, unless you're as lucky as I was, and are contacted by someone taking the targeted marketing approach (as described below). It took yours truly six years utilizing the passive approach to have the right woman find me.

There is not a lot of guidance to give on the passive approach, except to recommend a particular wine to sip while you wait, since you just sit back hoping those letters and postcards (or should I say emails and instant messages) arrive. The only real guidance that I can provide is in setting up your profile. The problem with the passive approach is that it reduces the chances of finding the right person by almost 80%, simply because you are not the one selecting the interviewees.

Mass Marketing

A number of people first turn to the mass marketing approach because they need to get their "Ya Ya's" out and gain a bit of experience in the dating world before they are ready to move on to a longer term relationship. This method involves writing to as many qualified "prospects" as possible in a short timeframe. The theory is that it's better to blanket cyberspace with mass mailings to which a small percentage of prospects will respond than to risk that nobody will respond to your targeted mailings. So if you send out form letters to 50 individuals, and you receive responses from just 20% of the "market," that's still 10 prospects! Now your biggest problem is figuring out how to juggle those 10 prospects, even though most of them will probably drop out rather quickly.

The biggest risk with this approach is that you'll saturate the market, leaving you with no more "leads" after your first round of mailings – no leads until more qualified candidates sign up for the site or other members return following relationships that didn't work out.

Sure, you can always contact these prospects again, assuming that you didn't receive a "Thank You but No Thank You" email. However, you can't keep writing to them indefinitely. At some point (probably after the third contact), you're going to move from being someone who follows up to being someone who's a nuisance. And if you continue writing, you will graduate to being viewed as a "stalker."

I am definitely not an advocate of this approach, either for dating or for finding a partner. The reason is that individuals who employ this approach try to set up interviews with as many people as possible. I have designated the term "Questing" for this type of approach. I'll discuss Questing later in a section called, "*An Interesting Transition.*" This approach is great for just having fun and meeting people. However, please be sure that the person you are meeting knows you are just out for a good time, not something serious.

I know, I know. You're saying, "Well, if I meet the right person, then I'll settle down." But this rarely happens using the mass marketing approach, for two reasons:

1. You are basing the contact list on superficial attributes such as: their looks, their looks and (possibly) their looks.

2. You won't give that person the time required in order to really get to know them, because you are simply meeting too many interviewees. Two and three interviews a day are not uncommon.

However, a lot of people do this, especially when they first begin to prospect.

Targeted Marketing

In my opinion, this is the only approach you should take once you have decided to be serious about finding the right person. Know up front that by taking this approach, you are not going to meet as many interviewees. You may not be on a date every night, let alone three a night. However, this is definitely the way to go once you are really ready to meet the right person.

If you begin your Internet Dating experience using the targeted approach and find that you're having relationships but haven't found the right person yet, don't give up. I repeat: Do not give up! Give yourself some time. You may well be on your way to finding the right person.

The targeted approach is the personal approach. The personal approach will not only help you establish a personal relationship more quickly, it will allow you to zero in on the perfect partner for you. I'm certain that most people would rather receive a short, but personalized note containing a compliment, asking a pertinent question or discussing common interests. I'd rather get a one- or two-sentence email that says, "I love snorkeling in the Florida Keys. Which of the reefs have you been to?" instead of a 500-word form letter.

If someone doesn't take the same amount of time and effort to write back with a personal email then it's probably best to move on. The same applies when you write to someone about a specific topic, or ask a specific question, and the person ignores what you wrote. For example, if you write an initial email discussing your mutual interest in snorkeling, and her response is, "Do you still have all your hair?" it's probably time to pursue someone else.

Another benefit (if you consider this a benefit) is not having so many prospective interviewees at one time that you require cheat sheets to keep track of them all. Believe me, this can and does happen. Fortunately, Marcia took this approach and found me. Note: while I suffered ☹ online for six years, she found the most wonderful man (me) in only one year. The Targeted Marketing approach really works.

Everybody's approach to prospecting is different. I'm sure most of you will choose your own path, depending on your needs and desires. At the end of the day, whatever works best for you is the best choice.

What to Expect

You usually receive the most responses when you first post your profile, assuming you've included a picture. I will not belabor the point anymore, but I cannot stress how important it is that you include a picture. Without a picture, others will assume the worst about you.

Even after being online for six years, I would still receive between five and 15 emails a week from women who saw my picture, read my profile and decided to initiate contact. Some were from Mass Marketers; some from Targeted Marketers. No matter how busy I was or how many emails I would get, I always tried to write back, even if it took a few days. It's basic respect. Fortunately, there's a good way to do this that will save you a lot of time.

By the way, although most people check their email regularly, sometimes many, many times each day, be aware that not everyone has time to check in as frequently. Some people have specific times, or even days of the week, when they catch up on their email. So don't be discouraged, and for goodness sakes, do not become frustrated or upset if someone doesn't respond to your note immediately.

How to Follow Up

If You're Not Interested

I may get into trouble if any of the women I responded to by saying "thank you but no thank you" read this. But, truth be told, I quickly realized that I couldn't respond to everyone with a personalized note. It would have taken too long. So, I created several "Thank You, but No Thank You" emails. Each had its own purpose. I used one if the woman lived outside my geographic dating range, and used a different one for prospects within my zip code. I used another if they met my criteria but I wasn't interested in them, and still another if they didn't meet my criteria at all. I might say that "I just met someone else, and I'm interested in seeing where it leads." Although these are rejection emails, they are polite and kind. I would never purposefully send anyone a hurtful email.

So, how should you respond? Let's start with the name. When you receive an Initial Contact email, you may only have the person's Internet name. Now, let's assume that you received an email from someone named XYZ. Here are two sample responses you could send to them. Depending on what you think about their profile, you may want to include the optional sentences, which I've enclosed in (parentheses).

To protect the innocent (me!), I have not included any of the actual emails that I wrote. That said, here they are:

The Sample "Geographically Undesirable" email:

Dear XYZ,

Thank you for taking the time to write me. I enjoyed reading your profile (and found you to be a very interesting person) [or] (and found that we have similar traits). However, at this time, I am looking to meet someone who lives closer to me. Good luck in your search.

The Sample "I Just Met Someone" email:

Dear XYZ,

Thank you for taking the time to write me. I enjoyed reading your profile (and found you to be a very interesting person) [or] (and found that we share similar traits). However, I recently met someone that I like, and we have decided to give this new relationship a chance. (Since we are still early in the relationship, would you mind if I wrote to you later if it does not work out?) Good luck in your search.

Using these two emails as templates, you can easily create your own. One invaluable piece of advice is to always reread your email before you click the send button.

If You Are Interested

Unfortunately, there is not a lot of guidance that I can give you here because when you are interested, you have to be yourself. Take the time to read the person's entire profile. Sometimes the writer will provide you more information about themselves in their email to you. This is especially so if your profile has indicated an interest that is not listed on their profile but they share that interest too. If they do and you find that they have other interests that you also enjoy, let them know that. Be yourself and if you like what you read, suggest a quick meeting. The reason for this is because in four out of five interviews, the interviewee will not be right for you. All for reasons that you won't even know about until you meet them. It is far better to eliminate an interviewee as early in the process as possible so that you can concentrate on meeting the right person for you.

4 Know Thyself

To know yourself
you have only to set down
a true statement of those that ever
loved or hated you.
— Johann Kaspar Lavater

When I first started dating, I just wanted to be accepted. Although I didn't realize this at the time, I do now. For the most part, we all have the similar wants, needs and desires. When a long-term relationship ends, we all go through pretty much the same stages. It doesn't matter if the relationship that ended was a 20- year marriage or a monogamous dating relationship that lasted only two years.

When your relationship ends, you may or may not know exactly what it is you desire from your next relationship or even whether you want another relationship right away. It's more likely that you'll know what you *don't* want the next time around. This is especially true if you've been through an abusive relationship. If you're not sure what you are looking for, don't worry: you're simply being honest with yourself.

Getting back into dating isn't exactly a 12-step plan, but there are certain waypoints you will have to pass on your journey toward your next (hopefully successful) relationship. Your wants, needs and desires will be determined by where you are at any given time on your journey. This is a constantly evolving process. Being honest and accepting of yourself is critical to your ability to select the right partner for yourself. That said, your first real relationship following your breakup will typically be the Transitional Dater.

Accepting the Transition

If you were married or were in a very long-term relationship, you will almost certainly go through a Transitional Relationship. Sometimes, if you're lucky, that Transitional Relationship will turn into a true non-Transitional Relationship. This is analogous to when an Initial Interview turns into a date.

I believe there are two types of Transitional Phases we go through. The first is the Transitional Dater, while the other is the proverbial Transitional Relationship. Each one exists less because it is right and more because it makes you feel good about yourself. They are both very good in their own ways. Why? Because feeling good about yourself allows you to gain self-confidence, and thus, in turn, allows you to seek a compatible relationship.

I have experienced both of these types in my life. The first was my Transitional Dater. I met my Transitional Dater online. She had placed an ad on one of the online services, and I responded. For the Initial Interview (I was still calling it a date back then), we decided to meet for dinner. I realized that she'd had at least one bad experience with someone who never showed up. I made that assumption because she asked me at least 10 times if I was really going to meet her. I wasn't about to let her down.

After exhaustive research, I estimated that I lived about an hour from our rendezvous point. I arrived two hours early, both because I didn't want to disappoint her and because I was very excited. In those two hours, I managed to scope out the restaurant, which took all of two minutes, and though I really had nothing to buy, I decided to kill time wandering through the nearby mall. After all, I could check out engagement rings just in case this went really well! The excitement of meeting her invigorated me to a point that I hadn't experienced in two decades. The shopping took all of 30 minutes. I now had only one hour and 28 minutes to kill.

As I explored the area, I saw a sign that led me to a particular part of this city that was supposed to be beautiful. It was only five miles away. Turns out, there were a few detour signs, which I followed. I'll bet you think you already know where this is leading. Well, you're wrong. After driving around the town, I followed the detour signs back, and ended up back at the restaurant with 53 minutes to spare. Did you really think that I was going to get lost and destroy this woman's trust in men for good? My saving grace is that I have a great sense of direction and I'm always on time. Sometimes I'm just way too early!

I entered the restaurant, just in case there was a line and I needed to put our names on a waiting list. It was only 5:07 PM, but I wanted to make sure that nothing would go wrong. It turned out that I was the first person there. I chatted with the hostess, explaining that this was my first date in about a million years. I sought out her opinion as to which dining room provided the best first-date ambiance. Together, we walked around the different dining areas, scoping out the best location. Once we made a decision, I asked her if she could hold that particular table for us. She promised to do her best. I now wonder how weird she thought I was and how sorry she felt for my date.

With 45 minutes left, I went to the bar and ordered a glass of wine. Although I sipped my wine very slowly, after emptying the glass there was still a good 35 minutes left before she was due to arrive. I declined another drink. As you may have come to realize by now, I'm a big believer in initial impressions. I located the proper seat, and reviewed what I was going to say. I looked at my watch: only 31 minutes left. I started to think about what a great relationship this might turn out to be. She loves to snow ski, and then it hit me that I didn't know anything more about her. But then again, what else did I need to know?

Finally, the time arrived: 6:00 ... then 6:05 ... and then my cell phone rang. She was running late, she apologized and asked if that was okay. I replied that it was no problem, as I had just arrived a few minutes earlier. The time was now 6:15 ... 6:30... Folks, I was dying here. She finally arrived at 6:45. When she entered the restaurant, I was in seventh heaven when I realized that I was actually attracted to her, unlike the blind date that was set up by my "so called" friends. A huge smile was plastered on my face when we said "hi," and we had a great dinner talking about skiing, etc. At the conclusion of the date we agreed to have dinner the following Saturday night.

We met Saturday evening, enjoyed dinner, and took a stroll around the strip mall. I put my arm around her.

Now, let me preface this by saying that I quit smoking in December of '86. I don't like smoke, and I can even smell it in my car when someone two cars ahead of me is smoking. I HATE IT!

Anyway, as we walked out of the restaurant, my dream woman pulled out a cigarette! I looked at her, she looked at me, and then she said she smoked only a few a day. Then she asked if it was okay, and continued saying that if someone didn't like that she smoked then it was their loss. I said to her, "I have no problem with it whatsoever," and we continued to walk with our arms around each other. But inside I started thinking, "What the heck did I just say?"

That was a long story, but it has a point.

I was just getting back into the game, and I was sorely lacking even one drop of dating self-esteem. So apparently, I was willing to break one of my cardinal rules simply because I was overjoyed to find anyone that I thought was attractive that also wanted to date me. As a footnote, since that time I have only met two people who smoked. The next one was a few months later, and I only considered dating her because she said she was going to quit on her birthday. She did, and still does not smoke to this day! She became my transitional lover and is still a friend.

The other woman who smoked just plain lied on her profile. She put down that she was a non-smoker. My profiles always stated that I was only interested in someone who didn't smoke. Anyway, we (the liar and I) went out and had a nice dinner. Following dinner, we went to a club to listen to music. After about an hour, I went to the little boy's room. When I returned and saw her smoking, I was totally in shock and immediately told her that it was time to leave. Needless to say, it was a very quiet ride back to her house. Later on in the book, I will discuss the safety reasons why you should not pick up, or be picked up, on the way to the Interview Date. One of the side benefits of not sharing a ride is that if the interview goes south, and many will, you are not forced to endure the other person's company in the potentially not-so-friendly confines of the car for the return trip.

There is nothing wrong about having one or two Transitional Relationships. Simply put, it's good. It's healthy and normal. Typically, one does not even realize, or willingly admit, to being in a Transitional Relationship – until you've been down the dating road awhile and have the ability to recognize situations for what they are. At that point, the only question that remains is if you do recognize a particular situation as not being a positive one, will you do anything about it? Too many times we allow bad relationships to continue simply because it's easier to remain in a bearable relationship than to cut it off and risk venturing, alone, into the unknown.

An Interesting Transition

The longer you date, the greater the likelihood is that you will encounter two additional types of transitions or phases. I've found that veteran online daters (including yours truly) often go through these. The first phase is called the "*Questing*" phase, and the second phase is the "*I Can Find Something Wrong with Everyone*" phase.

The "*Questing*" Phase usually takes place after a relationship has ended. As I said before, there is no easier place to meet lots of good, decent people than the Internet. In fact, there was a time when I had 11 interviews scheduled in 14 days! Deep down (I believe), Questing is a natural response to a fear of being alone, whereby the

Quester attempts to meet as many potential mates as possible and keep ALL options open.

I do not like or agree with the way some people go about Questing. I believe that if you meet someone you're interested in, such as Interviewee #8, you should take the time to get to know the person. I always want to give a newfound relationship the chance to succeed.

Whenever I started down that slippery "Questing Phase" slope, one of my best friends would rush to my side as I became infused with tremendous dating powers and was rapidly transformed into that incredible Superdater, "Questerman." She instantaneously became my sidekick, Hope.

Individuals begin their Questing by scheduling their interviews as though they were marathons. The main characteristic of genuine Questers is that they continue dating as many people as possible – even after meeting someone they really like.

Here's how it goes: They interview candidates 1 and 2, and reject both. Along comes number 3, and let's say they like this person. So, they set another date with number 3. They continue with interviews 4, 5, 6 and 7. Perhaps they like number 7. Well, they still go through with meeting 8, 9 and 10. So at this point, they are going on a third date with number 3, a second date with number 7, and they seem to like number 10. So a second date is planned with number 10. Number 7 gets taken off the list after the second date, and number 3 is heading for date number four. (Hmm, maybe I could create a scheduling software program just to juggle all this Questing. I bet I'd make millions.) Anyway, you get the idea.

I am also certain that many of you, especially women, probably like this idea. Ladies, before you jump all over me for singling out women, allow me to state the following: typically women do not pay for their Interview Dates, thereby making it easier and cheaper for them to Quest. Ladies, if you suddenly find yourself in the Questing phase, be sure that you don't make all your dates "dinner dates." If you do, you may need to start Questing at the gym several times a day just to keep off those extra pounds.

As described above, Questing definitely turns meeting so many people in such a short period of time into a veritable online "Meat Market." Tasting a couple of samples at the deli counter is one thing. Sampling too many types of meat at one time confuses the palate. I say if you find someone you like, give it a chance. If it doesn't work out, forget them and move on.

The "*I Can Find Something Wrong with Everyone*" phase also occurs after you've been dating and/or interviewing for a while. No matter how many people you meet, something is wrong with all of them. It could be as simple as you not liking the way they hold their utensils while they eat or the way they comb their hair. The significant symptom of this phase is being bothered by very minor things. If you find yourself in this phase, find a place to meditate and take an immediate break from Interviewing. When you return, you'll feel refreshed, and probably won't be (as) irritated by minor things like how they hold a fork, the color of their eyes, how they part their hair or that you happen not to like the aftershave or perfume they're wearing.

Baggage and Compatibility

For most people, dating is not just a way to meet friends and potential lovers, but is, without a doubt, a form of mental therapy. Dating is positively a great way to get rid of (at least some of) the emotional and psychological baggage you have accumulated through past (failed) relationships. These emotional scars can range from those that are merely quirky to (in some cases) problems that may be debilitating.

On the lighter side (or not), I know a woman who dated a man for several months. He always paused for several seconds after she finished a sentence before responding. Only after this pause would he reply to what she'd said. After a few dates, she joked about this habit, and the man's face turned bright red. It seemed that his ex-wife had bitterly complained that he was continually interrupting her. She complained so frequently about it that he got into the habit of pausing to make sure she had absolutely, positively finished speaking before he would utter a word.

On the darker side, remember Alan and Lisa, whose relationship I discussed in Chapter 1. After Lisa left town, Alan dissolved their business partnership. He later learned that she had been seeing a therapist for seven years to overcome a plethora of serious emotional problems. Chief among these was an intense fear of abandonment. It seems that, as a child, her parents were in the habit of taking unannounced vacations, sometimes for up to two weeks at a time. They left Lisa and her sister alone in the house to fend for themselves. As an adult, Lisa had come to realize that this fear was simply a vestige from her childhood, but whenever she attempted to repress that fear, it expressed itself through inexplicable and odd behavior (as we've seen).

Baggage and compatibility are important issues when it comes to choosing your dates. The two terms may even be synonymous when it comes to meeting, since we all have baggage. *That's right: we all have baggage.* In fact, baggage is an important aspect of compatibility.

Personally, I was simply looking for someone whose baggage did not fill an entire room. In fact, I would have preferred that her baggage fit under a table – not a dining room table, just a breakfast table. It wasn't that I was looking for someone without any issues. I was simply looking for someone with a comparable amount of baggage to mine. If you choose to be with someone who has significantly more or less baggage than you, then one of you may feel overwhelmed by the other's baggage. The lopsided distribution of baggage might cause additional stress on the relationship or even end it – unless, of course, you want to be a martyr. In this case, please consider professional help!

It is very unlikely that someone with a significant number of issues will tell you: "I simply have way too much to deal with. My life has been, and continues to be, unbearable. So, it's really best for both of us if you stay away." That's why you have to look for the signs that indicate that they have too much on their plate to make room for you. In the most severe cases, the overburdened individual will probably spill their guts to you during the Initial Interview. If that happens, you have two choices: either RUN or become friends.

Let's say that you meet someone and begin to develop a relationship. One day, the person you're dating tells you that she now realizes that she simply doesn't have enough time or energy for the relationship. So she tells you that she needs to end it. If this happens, please realize that this person really has way too much on her plate, a plate not large enough to hold both of you. Do the right thing and let her go. There are many profiles in the Internet Ocean, waiting to be caught by you. Do not become a *Glutton for Punishment in Shining Armor,* and if you think you may fall into this category, please pay attention to the upcoming *Knowing Who's Wrong for You* section.

One mid-summer evening, I received a phone call from Debbie, a friend of mine that I actually dated for awhile. Debbie told me the following story about her friend, Karen. It seemed that Karen had a friend who hadn't dated for awhile (for reasons I didn't learn about until later). Anyway, Karen felt that her friend, a single mother, really needed to get out more and meet some men. So one day while they were at the beach, Karen convinced this woman that she really did need to have a life outside of her kids and work.

Agreeing that maybe she should get out more, they left the beach and headed to Karen's house. They immediately fired up the computer, went online and began their Internet search for men. After viewing a number of candidates, they narrowed the field down to two men. They proceeded to print out both of their profiles, which included pictures. When she left Karen's house, she took the printouts to her car and promptly placed them in her bag, forgetting about them for the next month. Anyway, on the day that Debbie called me, Debbie, Karen and this woman were on the beach again with a dozen other single women.

At some point, the conversation turned to Internet Dating. This woman told the group that she and Karen had previously found two men on the Internet and had printed out their profiles. However, she wasn't sure what to do next, since she'd never pursued dating via the Internet before. She then realized that she still had both profiles in the bag she was carrying, and proceeded to dig them out.

Debbie took one look at the first profile and said…OMG that's Jon (yours truly). The woman started to ask Debbie this, that and the other thing about me, and after ascertaining that I was indeed handsome, intelligent and the all-around perfect gentleman, she asked Debbie if she thought I would want to meet her. This is what prompted her to call me that evening.

So, during the phone call, Debbie emailed me her picture and after one glimpse (man, was she hot!), I immediately asked when and where she wanted to meet. What happened next is that Debbie gave this woman my phone number. After three days of not hearing from this woman, I called Debbie and asked if the woman was still interested. She called her and reported back that:

1. She was very busy;
2. She was still very interested; and
3. She would call me soon.

About 10 days later she finally called. We met for drinks and decided to get together the following Saturday evening for dinner.

We conversed easily when we were together and definitely enjoyed each other's company. However, when we were apart, she never had time to speak with me either on the phone or online. It wasn't until after we went out a few times that she confided in me that her husband was murdered less than two years earlier.

Approximately six weeks into this relationship, I realized that while we really did like each other, the lack of communication caused me to feel that I was not as important to her as she was becoming to me. She was running around non-stop. She never rested. She never had time to talk. She always had to keep herself busy. This was what I observed. Maybe I was wrong, but I felt she hadn't given herself sufficient time to grieve for the tragic loss of her husband. While I'm not a therapist, I believe she simply was not ready for a real relationship at that point. So, I decided to stop dating her. She never understood why I wanted to end the relationship, and I couldn't bring myself to tell her what I really thought. We agreed to remain friends, but we quickly drifted apart. I truly believe that she will make a wonderful mate for someone when she's ready.

Beyond meeting people who are not ready for a steady relationship, you'll want to avoid people who are incapable of treating you as *you* – not as their ex-husbands, ex-wives, ex-girlfriends, etc. There is as much individual baggage on this planet as there are people, so listing every behavioral red flag would be pointless. Instead, I'll merely suggest that you avoid people whose behavior seems irrational and/or overly negative. For example, if your date is constantly snapping at you not to do "this or that" because her ex-boyfriend always did "this or that," it's probably best if you end the relationship.

I know of one woman who met her future husband just after he ended a long-term relationship. Week after week, the man would not stop talking about his ex-girlfriend, and he never ceased to compare his current date with his ex. Finally, the woman could stand it no longer, and broke things off – until such time, she told him, that he finally got over his ex. Six months later he was over his ex, so they got back together and they got married a few years later.

Knowing Who's Wrong for You

After a little more than a year of Internet Dating, I realized that I was meeting all the wrong people for all the wrong reasons. I kept repeating the same mistake over and over again. I suffered from the dreaded KISA Syndrome – also know as *Knight in Shining Armor* Syndrome.

Again, I'm not a psychologist, but I do believe that being attracted to someone who has more baggage than you makes you feel, at least subconsciously, better about yourself. Their problems/issues allow you to forget about your own problems/issues and concentrate on solving theirs.

Ultimately, there's nothing wrong with being someone's Knight in Shining Armor, but it has to be for the right reasons. That is, you should not deliberately seek to be a KISA. If you happen to stumble into it, that's fine. It's about who you truly are, not who you attempt to turn yourself into. Wow, that sounds like a great statement on life in general! Anyway, a Knight in Shining Armor may simply be a person with an overly caring disposition.

When I first started dating, I found myself attracted to women who had lots and lots of baggage. For hours on end I would listen to their problems and I would try to help solve them. It made me feel great that I was helping someone. I enjoyed being their Knight in Shining Armor.

Since you may have already figured out that I enjoy telling stories, here is my Knight in Shining Armor story – at least the one to which I'm willing to confess. I'll take the other KISA story to the grave with me!

This particular episode occurred several months into my Internet Dating adventures. In case you're keeping track, I met this particular woman between my Transitional Dater and my Transitional Relationship, in a chat room. She lived about 600 miles away, and like me (at the time), she was separated. We instantly hit it off, exchanged pictures, and chatted some more. After about an hour of chatting, we spoke on the phone and really, really liked each other. We were, more or less, in the same situation, and we both had children around the same ages. Everything sounded good ... no, everything sounded great ... at the time!

We talked by phone several times a day, and we constantly chatted online. This went on for several weeks. One day, she told me she had plans to visit a friend of hers over the holidays, and we talked about the two of us getting together. As the holidays approached we agreed on a date to meet.

The week before she was to come up, I asked her for her friend's phone number. After all, I wanted to talk to her once she arrived. All of a sudden, I came face to face with one of those proverbial pregnant pauses. After the pause, she explained that she'd previously met someone online who was recently widowed. They were both very depressed and overwhelmed with the approaching holidays. Prior to our meeting online, she had already agreed to spend the holidays with this other man. She thought she would be performing a good deed, helping him get through the holidays, sort of a female version of a Knight in Shining Armor...perhaps a Mother Teresa in Shining Armor??? She assured me this was purely a platonic relationship and then asked me not make a big deal out of it.

The day before we were going to meet, she called and told me she had to cancel. What may appear to be platonic in one person's eyes may well be love in another's eyes. She began telling me what a big mistake she'd made by coming, that this other person turned out to be crazy in love with her. She said that he made her so uncomfortable that she'd considered leaving several times, but in the end, decided to stay. I became concerned, but I respected her wishes.

A few days later (the night before my son and I were to fly to Florida to be with family for the holidays), I received a panicked phone call from this woman. My son and I were scheduled to be on an 11:30 AM flight from Baltimore-Washington International (BWI) Airport. It was now 8:30 PM the night before. We lived about a three-hour drive from the airport. The woman told me that this other man had started to become verbally abusive when she was unable to reciprocate his love. She realized that she needed to leave. She packed her bags, but when she tried to leave he wouldn't let her out of his home. I told her to call a taxi and just leave. About 9:15 PM she called back, hysterical. She had finally called a taxi, but the man subsequently called the cab company back and cancelled it.

"That's it," I said, "I'm coming to get you and I'm not taking no for an answer." She said no and hung up. I tried to call her cell phone once again, but there was no answer. I began to think that maybe one of us should call the police, but I had no idea where she was, except that she was in some town on Long Island. Moreover, she had called from a phone that was programmed to automatically block the Caller ID.

Finally, around 10 PM, she called back. She kept changing her mind about whether she was going to stay or leave. She told me that she thought the man was listening in on the conversation, and promised she would call me right back. Around 10:30 PM, the phone rang again. Once again she was hysterical. I said, "That's it! If you can't get out of the house, I'm going to come and get you out." I told her to call me in 15 minutes.

The area where I lived did not have very good cell phone coverage at the time. The 15 minutes would allow me enough time to leave the house and drive far enough to get to an area where my cell phone consistently worked. I was on my way to the heart of Long Island to rescue this Damsel in Distress. I had no idea where I was going (besides out of my mind), since I had never in my life driven farther east on Long Island than Kennedy International Airport (JFK).

The area where I lived did not have very good cell phone coverage at the time. The 15 minutes would allow me enough time to leave the house and drive far enough to get to an area where my cell phone consistently worked. I was on my way to the heart of Long Island to rescue this Damsel in Distress. I had no idea where I was going (besides out of my mind), since I had never in my life driven farther east on Long Island than Kennedy International Airport (JFK).

It was almost 11 PM when my cell phone rang. I told her that I was on my way and asked her to check in with me every 15 minutes or so, more often if she needed to. After about 15 minutes, I was on the New Jersey Turnpike heading north. Unfortunately, I was concentrating on her situation more than my driving, and I missed my turnoff. (I thought to myself, "This is going ... just wonderful, so far.") I had to be on a plane out of BWI in 12 hours, and I was headed in the wrong direction at 65 miles per hour.

Once I realized that I'd missed my exit, I took the next exit, and really, really tried to make a quick turn around. Unfortunately, though not surprisingly, I ended up taking a short tour of Newark, NJ. Finally, after a seemingly endless number of on and off ramps, I made my way back onto the Turnpike, and was heading south. Now, concentrating more on my driving and less on her situation, I located and took the correct exit for the Goethals Bridge and Staten Island, home of the malodorous Fresh Kills landfill. From there, it's a straight shot to the Verrazano Bridge and into Brooklyn. Hopping on the Belt Parkway, it's another 30 minutes or so to JFK, which would include a pit stop at a gas station smack dab in the median of the Parkway. Once past JFK, I really had no idea where I was going or for that matter, what the heck I was doing. Should I really have involved myself in this mess? Should I have just seen it for what it was – none of my business – and walked away?

While I was stopped at the gas station, I consulted my trusty map. Knowing only the name of the town where she was staying, I decided my best route of travel would be to continue on the Belt Parkway and take it to the Southern State Parkway. I always wondered where the Southern State led to. In a matter of two short months, I would find out that it led to where my Transitional Lover lived.

Allow me a moment to digress... About 20 years earlier, I remembered looking at a map of Long Island and noticed that there were two parallel highways that made their way up Long Island. They were the Northern State Parkway and the Southern State Parkway. I never really understood why they were given these names, since neither one had anything to do with where they were located with respect to each other. Yes, the Southern State Parkway was indeed in the southern portion of the state yet the Northern State Parkway was also in the southern part of the state. Doesn't make sense to me, but then again I was born and bred in Chicago. If it had been up to me, I would have named them the Northern Island Parkway and the Southern Island Parkway. Just seems to make more sense. I can hear the traffic reporters now referring to them as the N.I.P. and the S.I.P. Together, they actually sound like they could be a hit TV show: NIP and SIP – about two cosmetic surgeons that meet at New York City's most exclusive club after a day of surgeries. (By the way, I demand payment for these rights if anyone uses this idea for a TV show or book.)

Anyway, back to the story. The woman called back to tell me that she was finally able to leave the house, and had found her way to a 24-hour eating establishment. She wasn't exactly sure where she was or how to get there. So she asked someone who worked there for directions, and they told me to look for a particular road. I was told this just as I was about to pass that road's exit. Quickly changing lanes, I somehow made it to the exit. I went down the road and by some miracle I found the place. She was standing with her suitcase, outside in the rain, in tears.

I leapt off my horse... I mean out of the car, and put her suitcase in the back seat. We talked, and she began to calm down. By now, it was almost 1:30 AM. I had 10 hours until my plane was scheduled to leave from an airport almost five hours away. I asked her for her tickets, called the airline from my cell phone, and made arrangements for her to be on the first flight out of LaGuardia Airport. She had five hours until her flight. When all that was settled, we looked at each other and started to make-out.

Suddenly, I realized that I needed to get back home to shower, pack, wake up my son (that can be an adventure in itself) and drive to BWI, which is actually past downtown Baltimore. I didn't have time to drive her to LaGuardia. Maybe I could have, but neither one of us knew how to get there from where we were. So we drove to JFK to find a taxi. Around 4:30AM, after a bit more necking, we found the only cab that appeared to be in the entire airport that night. We said goodbye, and I made sure she had money for the fare. Then I followed her cab until I reached my exit for the Belt Parkway, and headed to back to New Jersey. I was her Knight in Shining Armor.

Exhausted, I made it to BWI with my son. As it turned out, our flight was actually an hour later than I thought, so we arrived with plenty of time to spare. I slept for about 30 minutes on the flight to Florida. Later that afternoon, I received a call from my Damsel, confirming my Knighthood status.

After a while, we both realized we really had very little in common. In addition, I began to see that she had a myriad of other issues. She drove up to visit me, and I flew down to visit her. After two weeks it was over. Regardless of what happened (or didn't happen), I knew that if someone needed that kind of help again, I would be on my way in a heartbeat.

About a year later, after explaining to a close friend the type of women I was meeting, she suggested that I read a particular book that discussed why we choose the wrong people. One chapter described my Knight in Shining Amour Syndrome (KISAS) to a tee. I didn't even need to read further than the first couple of chapters before it clicked, and I realized that I had to put an end to my KISAS. I haven't had the Knight problem since. While I will try to help anyone, I no longer considered a person like the woman above as someone with whom I would seek a relationship. As I've already said before, one's baggage should fit under the table.

Note: If you have already started or are a member of a local *OCOCDA* Chapter, you may want to consider starting a special interest group for those that suffer from *KISAS*.

Other Syndromes of Interest:

I Cannot Sit At Home Alone Syndrome

This is definitely an area of concern. I have learned that a major red flag should be raised if you are with someone who stays so busy that they don't have time for you. I know. You might be saying to yourself, "Well, if this person really wanted to be with me, they would make the time." That's probably true in 90% of cases, but not all of the time. It's that 10% that I am cautioning you about. Some of these people seem to be running around like a chicken with its head cut off. Others simply cannot sit at home alone. I believe that in both of the cases I encountered, the women had some very serious issues that had not been resolved. I am certain that they were not even aware that they were acting this way. It was obvious to not only myself, but to others.

It seems to me that people must first be content with themselves before they can hope to be in successful relationships.

Needy Men and the Women Who Mother Them Syndrome

This syndrome is best explained with an example. A few years ago, one of my friends met a woman (an actress) online, who suggested that they have their Interview Date following a play she was appearing in that Saturday night. My friend was love-struck as soon as his "date" appeared onstage (talent is a powerful aphrodisiac), and their dinner was wonderful. There was an immediate, and mutual, physical attraction, and plenty of common interests to talk about. Several dates later, the woman revealed that her ex-boyfriend was calling her dozens of times a day, begging her to return. She'd left him because he'd cheated on her, but now that he was literally pleading, crying and confessing that he couldn't live without her, she found herself strangely attracted to him once again.

To make a long story short, the woman dumped my friend, even though she acknowledged to him that this was probably a mistake. She said, "My ex needs me. I need to take care of him," and that ... was the end of that. Obviously, this syndrome will work in your favor if you're a needy man or the kind of woman who's compelled to nurture the seemingly helpless. If you really are one of these needy folks, please seek professional help! Otherwise, run like hell if you meet either of these two types of personalities.

Women Who Like "Bad Boys" Syndrome

Yes, there are men who like "Bad Girls," but I've found that women who like "Bad Boys" are much more common. In many cases, you can easily spot the woman who likes "Bad Boys" because she'll immediately admit to it. She'll also admit that she'd be much better off establishing a loving relationship with a man who is intelligent, kind and mature, and that you fit that bill. But no matter how hard she tries to make a go of it with you, she'll return to the "Bad Boys" sooner or later. You "Bad Boy-loving" ladies know the type: these guys call when it's convenient for them, stand you up, and ALWAYS treat you like dirt.

After running into a "Bad Boy-lover," some of you men may feel compelled to become a "Bad Boy" yourself. However, it won't really last unless you *really* are that type of individual. You're much better off being who you are and seeking a more mature individual to date.

People Who Date Considerably Younger and/or Older Candidates Syndrome

Don't get me wrong. There's absolutely nothing unhealthy about dating people who are 10, 20 or even 30 years younger or older than you are, provided of course that:

1. You aren't dating my daughter, and

2. You're not dating children.

Some May-September or October-April relationships produce wonderful results. But in general, extreme age differences are less likely to facilitate lasting relationships because… well, you're both at very different stages in your lives. In most cases, it's the women I know of who suffer from pursuing younger men.

I can think of several examples of women in their late thirties and forties, very interested in getting married or having children, who persist in dating men in their mid-twenties – men with no interest in settling down any time soon. Well, on the other extreme, I also know a number of men who have dated women 20 to 30 years younger. For example, there are both men and women, 55 years and older who will state in their profiles that their dating range is someone from 25 to 35 years old. My dating range was from about 5 years younger to about 2 years older than my age, but then again, I was really looking for the love of my life. I can't begin to tell you the number of women who told me how refreshing it was to find a man whose dating-age range was realistic.

How to Identify Who is Right for You

While it's possible, of course, for people from very different backgrounds to meet, fall in love, and stay in love, it's far more likely that a relationship will flourish when both individuals:

- Come from the same economic background.
- Are raised with the same values.
- Are intellectual equals.
- Are both, for the most part, happy individuals.
- Share the same outlook on life.
- Share some of the same activities and/or hobbies.
- View childrearing the same way.
- Share the same manners.
- Are equally clean or sloppy in regards to how they maintain their home.
- Are encumbered with the same amount of emotional/psychological baggage.

In general, both parties must share a complementary amount of baggage for things to work out in a positive way. It's also possible for people carrying a lot of baggage or different quantities of baggage to form solid relationships, just maybe not healthy relationships. In the end, the best relationships are founded on shared values, interests and a mutual attraction.

In fact, the best relationships are created when neither person in the relationship *needs* the other!

Even if you are in a Geographically Desirable relationship, and even if you see each other on a regular and spontaneous basis, most people will not feel relaxed enough to really, completely be themselves with the other person for at least six months to a year. My advice is to give your relationship at least a full year before you make any significant changes to your life. While I can't guarantee anything in life, giving your relationship this amount of time should allow you to know this individual for who he/she really is – assuming he or she has nothing major to hide (and most people don't).

In addition, there are a few more points I would like you to consider and apply as you see fit:

- Be very wary if you are asked by anyone to loan them money, to cosign a loan or otherwise put yourself financially on the line for them. Don't be taken in.

- Remember, if something or someone appears too good to be true, they may very well be. Don't kid yourself.

- There is nothing wrong with running a background and credit check, just to be sure.

- I might be suspicious if I never meet any of their parents, siblings or children.

- I would definitely be suspicious if a number of their small stories don't add up, especially if they keep telling you that it's nothing or that you're imagining things. Be certain.

- If you ever find yourself making excuses for the person you're dating, then quite possibly you are dating the wrong person.

Conclusion

If you find yourself always meeting the wrong kinds of people, I would suggest the following. First, try to examine what the common traits are that these people possess. Next, create a "Criteria Checklist." List both the traits you are looking for and those you want to avoid. Finally, make a serious effort to avoid people with the negative traits, and only consider interviewing those that possess the positive traits. If you think you can't, well, just look at me! I quit smoking, which means I can do anything! If avoidance alone does not solve the problem, then find and read some books on the subject. Talk to friends about it. Finally, consider professional help, because if you are unable to break this cycle it can become very unsettling and possibly lead you to question your own self worth.

5 Your Next Step

Do Not Attempt to Adjust the Dials: You Have Entered the "BII Zone"

The BII Zone, otherwise known as the "Before Initial Interview" Zone, is not to be confused with the B2 zone (whatever the heck that may be). The BII Zone is that point in time between your initial contact and the first "Interview." Okay, so I just made up this term, but I needed something to describe exactly what takes place during this phase of the mating dance.

By now, you've made initial contact (probably by email) with someone whose picture you've seen online, or someone with whom you've privately exchanged pictures. You think you're attracted to this person, and he or she sounds compatible. Now, here's what I believe is the single most important piece of advice I can offer, besides the safety tips: **Meet and interview your potential mate as soon as possible**. In fact, this chapter could have consisted entirely of that one statement. However, it's unlikely that anyone new to Internet Dating will take my advice. So read on and use the suggestions that seem right for you.

Suggested Route

Here's an interesting statistic to keep in mind: only about one in five carefully screened Initial Interviews will actually lead to a real date. My suggestion is that once you meet the person, you should either commit to dating them or find someone more appropriate.

I'm sometimes asked if there's such a thing as rushing into a face-to-face meeting. My answer is always and emphatically "No!" As long as both parties are interested in meeting, there's no reason to wait. I can't begin to count how many times people have told me that they've spent weeks, even months, exchanging emails and talking on the telephone. After that amount of time, special feelings are established, but these feelings can evaporate within a nanosecond at the first face-to-face meeting. If there's no physical attraction, 99.999% of the time, it's over right then and there.

How should you proceed? First, send a nice email in response to the person's initial contact. Here's a sample:

> *Dear XYZ,*
>
> *Thank you for taking the time to write me. I enjoyed reading your email, and feel that we share a number of common interests. I would like to know more about you. I would prefer to speak on the phone, and would be happy to give you a call. What do you think?*

Note: If you receive a note like this and you are not comfortable giving out your phone number, then write the person back, saying you would be more comfortable calling them, and would they please send you their phone number.

Also, if you have any questions about the person that were not answered in the user profile, you may want to include them in this initial communication. For example, maybe you are curious about the ages of their children or an aspect of their religious beliefs. You might as well ask now! Basically, it's at this point, the BII point, that you can ask the tough questions and/or raise potentially thorny issues – if you have any. The reason for this is that once the relationship begins, you may be apprehensive about asking these types of questions. I'm not advocating that you subject this person to the third degree (that, in and of itself, should raise a red flag in the other person's mind), but don't be afraid to ask questions. The longer you wait, the harder and more awkward it will be to ask the tough questions later on.

In the email above, I suggested a phone conversation. Again, because your security is important, let me briefly review the rules:

> Do not give out your last name, your home phone number, your place of employment and especially your home address to anyone. Do not have any identifying information on your voicemail. Period!

If you give out your home phone number, there are online reverse lookup websites that can provide your address based on that information. If the person says you can call them, then by all means do so, but always take the following precautions:

- Use your cell phone.

- Dial *67 before dialing their number. This hides your phone number from the Caller ID of the person you are calling.

If you ignore my advice and choose to give out your phone number (and I strongly suggest you don't), then only give out your cell phone number, and absolutely, positively do *not* include any identifying information on your voicemail, including information that identifies where you work.

Once you speak with the person by phone (assuming they sound like a nice person; someone you would like to meet), set up an Initial Interview as soon as possible. Then, meet face to face in a very public place!

There have been times when I've received either an initial contact note or corresponded with someone in a chat room, talked on the phone and then met in-person – all within the space of two hours. These experiences have been fun and exciting. Just like the Internet, Internet Dating can move at the speed of light.

However, due to timing constraints and people's busy schedules, children, etc., most Initial Interviews cannot take place that quickly. As a guideline, the time between speaking on the phone and the Initial Interview should be only a few days, or a week at the most.

In the next chapter we'll talk about what will happen (or not) during that all-important first meeting.

6 Your First Meeting

It's Showtime

When it comes to the Initial Interview, you need to follow a few simple rules intended to keep you safe rather than sorry. There are definite do's and don'ts when it comes to your first meeting. I also have included a section on dating etiquette, as well as a short discussion on explosive chemistry! By the way, this explosive chemistry has absolutely nothing to do with blowing up high school science labs.

During the course of my Internet Dating career, I developed my own set of rules and guidelines. So, in the following two chapters, I'll share those rules, etiquette and the do's and don'ts that have served me well.

If it weren't for the small percentage of jerks that ruin the reputation of the entire male gender in the eyes of some women, the following rules would be unnecessary. I recognize that some women also taint the reputation of the female gender, but personal safety is not usually the main concern for men.

Meeting Rule #1: Meet only in a very public place!

While I'm certain that everyone knows this rule and a lot of people, especially veteran online daters, recognize just how important this rule is, not everyone actually adheres to it – especially first-time Internet daters. For your safety, you must meet in a public place. The location of your Initial Interview can be a restaurant, bar, coffee shop, bookstore or anywhere else, as long as it's in a public setting where other people are nearby. Do *not* meet in the parking lot of the restaurant where your Interview Date is going to take place: meet inside! Always park your car in a visible area, as close to the main entrance as possible, and if you are meeting at night, park under a working light.

I specifically mention parking lots due to an experience a friend of mine had when she failed to follow Rule #1. This occurred as she was on her way to her first-ever Initial Interview. In her defense, this occurred back in the late 90's before there was a vast pool of knowledge on how to approach Internet Dating. It turned out that she was not familiar with the restaurant where they were going to meet. So the person she was meeting suggested that they rendezvous in a parking garage along the way to the restaurant. He explained that this would be a good idea in case one of them was running late. That way, the other could park and wait. Once they both arrived, she could follow him to the restaurant in her car. He suggested, and she agreed, that they meet at the top level of the parking garage. This should have been her first warning sign!

When she arrived at the designated parking lot, there was no one else around except for the person she was meeting. The guy came out of his car, she rolled down the window, and they started talking. Everything seemed okay up to this point. She was about to step out of the car when, suddenly several cars arrived and tried to box her in. The guy grinned, saying he had a few friends with him. Thank goodness my friend realized what was going on. She immediately hit the accelerator and got out of there.

Again, let me remind you that, as a rule, the vast majority of people you will meet online are, if nothing else, safe. It's that tiny percentage you need to be aware of. The jerk who orchestrated the parking lot plot was someone she met in a chat room, not through an Internet Dating service. I've already mentioned the benefits of Internet Dating sites versus chat rooms, so let this example be one more thing in their favor. Please keep in mind that chat rooms provide complete anonymity and therefore, they are potentially more problematic. On the other hand, the very nature of Internet Dating services encourages people to be more honest.

Meeting Rule #2: Don't be picked up at your house

This is a variation of my rule on not giving out your address. Good advice, in the beginning, but at some point, I would hope that you establish enough trust to reveal the location of your home. I've picked up my Interview Dates at their homes on a few occasions, but since I'm not a psycho stalker, none of the women had anything to fear.

Each time this has happened, I've always asked the women why they provided me with their home address. The answer was always that same: their gut instincts told them

I was okay. Ladies, please do not trust your gut instincts. Drive yourself, especially if you have children residing in your home! It's best to err on the side of caution.

Meeting Rule #3: Stay out of the other person's car

Okay, so now you've arrived at the interview location in separate cars, but since the interview is going well, the Initial Interview turns into a date, and the two of you decide to continue this budding romance elsewhere. Please, PLEASE, take separate cars to the new location! After all, if the interview ends up going south, do you really want to be cooped up with the other person for as long as it takes to get to where you left your car? Maybe the other person has a drinking or anger (or whatever) problem that has not yet revealed itself. As a rule, do not share a car until at least the second, or preferably, the third date. Certainly do not get into someone's car until you are comfortable doing so.

Meeting Suggestion: Hatch an emergency escape plan

The biggest cliché in the Western Dating World is the man who, after sleeping with the woman on the first date, immediately announces that he has to get up early to play tennis, golf, racket ball, etc., or attend an important early-morning client meeting. This tip allows you to put a creative twist on that cliché. There are two basic ways to approach this, and any number of minor variations.

Strategy #1 is to inform your date up front that you have to be somewhere else by a certain time. Preferably, you should tell your interviewee about this the day before you actually meet. The trick is making sure the reason for being somewhere else is something that can be postponed or cancelled, just in case the interview turns into a date.

If you have children, for example, you might tell your date that you have to pick up your son or daughter from a friend's house by 9:00 PM. If you're a professional, you could claim that you're expecting an important business call at a particular time. If things go badly, you've got the perfect "out." Be sure to bring your cell phone with you. That way, when things go well, you can check your messages and discover that your son or daughter ended up catching a ride with someone else, or that the important business call was postponed.

Strategy #2 is to (again) bring your cell phone with you on the date, and arrange for a friend to call you about 33 minutes (30 minutes would be too obvious) into the date. This friend will have an "emergency," if need be, that you must attend to. Personally, I don't like this option, because anyone who's seen enough television will recognize that this is a blatant ruse to shorten the Interview Date. Of course, I suppose it's better than telling your date that you can't stand their presence, and as I've previously stated, I'm a firm believer in being polite.

Do's and Don'ts

Do not talk about your previous relationships, especially if you have nothing positive to say about them. Remember, the first meeting is like a job interview. When I interview candidates for a job, I usually ask about their previous work experience. If all they do is complain, I think, "Well, I certainly don't want this person working for me." The same holds true during the Initial Interview.

I've had a number of women pour their hearts out to me about past relationships. One woman even told me how she met a married man and had an affair with him. She was in love and ended her marriage for him. For six years, he kept telling her the proverbial fib about leaving his wife. Of course, he never did. Take careful note here: this is another major RED FLAG! Even I took note of this one, despite the fact that I was in my Knight in Shining Armor phase.

Be sure to pay attention to your date and what they are saying. However, **do not** actually take notes while on an interview. A friend of mine freaked out a bit when the person she was meeting pulled out a pen and notepad. He actually began taking notes! I asked why she didn't simply just tell him not to do that, or why she didn't get up and leave. She said that he seemed timid and harmless, and she didn't want to hurt his feelings. If YOU are the one who took the notes when you met my friend, STOP TAKING NOTES! It freaks people out.

If you don't feel an instant rapport with your interviewer or interviewee, **do** be nice. Enjoy the drink, have a nice conversation and then move on. While you may be tempted to get up and leave right away, please don't! There's no excuse for being rude.

Limit your Interview Dates to a cup of coffee, a drink or a glass of water – okay, maybe not a glass of water. Note I said, "A", as in *one* drink. Too many drinks can seriously impair your judgment. The dangers of IUI, "Interviewing Under the Influence," are especially perilous when the person you're meeting to interview is "border line."

Let's say you meet someone who is really nice. You converse easily but at the same time there is no "real" chemistry. So you decide to stick around awhile enjoying the art of verbal repartee, while the two of you continue to consume several more drinks. Well, after a drink (or three), they seem eminently more qualified then they did 20 minutes earlier. This can lead to a major mistake that you definitely do not want to make during an Initial Interview.

In addition, by limiting the Initial Interview to only a drink or a cup of coffee, you are not locking yourself into an entire evening of planned and/or ticketed events before you actually meet the other person. I know a guy who, in an effort to impress his potential mates, would reserve the best table at expensive restaurants and Broadway theater tickets for the first date. I can't tell you how many times he and/or his interviewee endured four to six hours of boredom simply because they'd locked themselves into a long, unbearable Interview Date.

Do dress appropriately for your Interview Date. You needn't wear a tuxedo or evening gown when meeting for a drink or ice cream, but it's important to demonstrate that you're taking the Interview seriously enough to put some time and thought into what you've worn. At a minimum, common sense dictates that you'll want to look your best for the other person. I met and dated a woman who interviewed a different guy the night before we met. She blew him off completely because he wore sandals with black socks.

Of course, there's no accounting for individual taste and, in some instances, individual taste may determine whether the relationship will move forward or not. Even how you dress can be a determining factor as to whether there is chemistry or not! My friend who took women to fancy restaurants and Broadway shows on first dates was once mortified when his online date showed up wearing nothing but a long T-shirt and sandals for the theater. "I wear more than that to the beach," he later complained. Needless to say, this woman didn't pass her Interview. For that matter, she probably was not attracted to his dressing attire either.

Finally, please be aware of one essential "Do." **Do** be aware that you may encounter a scam artist or "unbalanced" individual along the way. Yes, these people do exist, though you're less likely to meet one than you might think, especially if you watch certain television shows, particularly the news. They would like you to think that that 98% of Internet users are sexual predators or identity thieves.

Here's my rule of thumb: If you wouldn't give certain information to a total stranger on the street, don't give that information to someone you've been chatting with online until you get to know them very, very well.

Explosive Chemistry

I'm not going to say much about my experiences (or lack thereof) on this subject, simply because my children, parents, new in-laws and others who think they know me, will read this book

This section could easily have been placed in the Common Mistakes Chapter. However, if this issue does arise, it usually rears its ugly head, pun intended, when the Initial Interview turns into a date and a few too many drinks are consumed. If necessary, go back to the Introduction chapter and reread the section on MUI (Meeting Under the Influence) or the above section discussing IUI (Interviewing Under the Influence). The initial violation of this rule should cost both offenders their Questing Privileges for one month.

That said, there is a positive side to explosive chemistry. If both parties are physically passionate AND have something more in common than ... well, just physical passion... it can make for the kind of relationship that's seen in the movies more than it's experienced in real life. But it's not likely – probably just a good "rebound" will ensue – which may not be bad for someone just out of a bad relationship or marriage. Remember: don't forget the Latex, just in case you get lucky.

7 Common Mistakes

The endeavor to love is never a mistake.

Basic Dating Etiquette

While entire books have been written about etiquette, most do not even touch the subject of dating etiquette. If they do then they may only contain the very basic rules of dating etiquette. So here, I offer you mine. It's okay if you don't agree with my suggestions. However, please keep in mind that these etiquette tips are only for the Initial Interview Date. Once you've fallen in love, all's fair.

- **Don't** feel compelled to confess your deepest, darkest secrets, fears and phobias. We all have dark secrets, fears and phobias, but sharing them is part of getting to know another person. Save the worst for later, when it hopefully won't completely terrify the other person.

- **Don't** talk with your mouth full.

- **Don't** get sloppy drunk or talk about your experiences of being sloppy drunk.

- **Don't** burp, fart, vomit, etc. These are usually "deal killers."

- **Don't** be rude or condescending to waiters, bartenders, coat check girls, valets, etc.

- **Don't** talk about sex, unless the subject arises.

- **Don't** talk about your "ex" unless the subject arises, and then be very careful what you say and how you say it.

- **Don't** talk about how "hot" this or that person is, unless the subject arises.

- **Don't** bring up politics or religion unless that's one of the reasons you two got together in the first place.

- **Do** be polite, without being obnoxious.

- If you're having a terrible time, **don't** make it obvious. There are enough hurt feelings in this world. Rolling your eyes or staring at the "cute" guy or girl at the next table is rude and inexcusable.

- If you're having a great time, **do** make it obvious. Touch the person on the shoulder or arm, smile, and tell them you're having a great time. Women, this is important! Most men have no clue when a woman likes him, unless the woman makes it *painfully* obvious. This may seem silly to you, but ladies, PLEASE make it painfully obvious.

Okay, now that I've discussed some (but not all) very basic etiquette, here are a few more suggestions.

- **It's not all about you!** Yes, you'll want to bring up your life and times, but if this relationship is destined to become "THE ONE," you don't need to submit an exhaustive oral biography during the first 30 minutes of the interview.

- **Stop selling yourself.** Now that you've earned the all-important Interview Date, relax and be yourself. Your date has already demonstrated that they are interested enough to have dinner, drinks, coffee, etc. with you. You don't have to whip out brochures, customer testimonials and money-back guarantees to convince them that you're the greatest guy or gal. It's a waste of time trying to "prove" that you're the best mate on the planet. Your date will decide that.

- **Listen and ask questions.** If you are genuinely interested in what your date has to say, listening and asking questions will come naturally. If you're not, fake it, and then resolve to find someone else. If you're interested in what your date has to say, but you can't think of any questions and can only talk about yourself, seek therapy.

- **Please see above and DO NOT spend the entire time together talking about yourself.** Relationships are not one way, and there is nothing more boring than a lecture. Enough said.

- **Don't refer to yourself in the third person.** Now you may think that people who refer to themselves in the third person exist only in certain television shows, but there are more than a handful of real-life examples.

  One woman I know of tried to date a man who did this, but quickly tired of statements such as, "If you'd like to get to know the real Ted, you'll find that you need to dig deep" and "Ted likes to be spoiled, with back rubs and foot massages, but he's not looking for a Harem girl." Thanks, Ted, for those important tips.

- **Don't refer to yourself as the royal "We."** Okay, this isn't very common but it does happen. Individuals who refer to themselves as "we" are usually people who've been in long-term relationships and have hopefully, only temporarily, lost their identities in couple-hood.

  I know of one woman who, after 15 years of marriage, automatically said things like, "We don't eat at Japanese restaurants very often" or "We don't like films with gratuitous nudity." Within a year of being divorced, she got over this problem, especially after her friends kept pointing it out.

- **Calm your nerves.** It's natural to be nervous and anxious about getting back into the dating scene, but please realize that if your first interview doesn't work out, you'll have many more opportunities. If you're shy, resist the temptation to loosen your inhibitions (too much) by getting smashed on vodka martinis before your applicant even arrives for their Interview.

Other people get so nervous that they lose control over their voice level. A friend once dated a woman who was literally shouting in a quiet café without realizing it. Another friend who, unlike me, doesn't mind dating smokers had to draw the line when his Interview Date excused herself every 10 minutes to suck down a cigarette. She claimed that it was because her nerves were so frayed. People, people, it's an Interview Date, not a summons to the Spanish Inquisition!

My Commandments

A relationship should be a positive thing in your life. Feeling bad or having to walk on eggshells is not a good habit to get into. Over the past few years, I've learned what I can deal with and what I cannot deal with. As a result, I've developed my four commandments that are essential for my own mental health. They are:

1. I shall not be with someone that does not understand that children come first.

2. I shall not be lied to.

3. I shall not be with a self-centered individual.

4. I shall be with someone who communicates.

First Commandment: Thy Children Come First

This commandment is really all about being a good parent. A parent needs to be able to balance their life between children, work, hobbies, extracurricular activities and the person they are dating.

Remember, children of different ages have different needs, so take your child's age into account when considering this commandment. Above all, children should never feel threatened or fear that their parent's friend will take away their parent's love for them. There are plenty of books on this subject, and I recommend you browse through some of them.

As for me, one of the most important aspects of a relationship is whether the other person understands my needs as a parent. I need to know that if I'm dating someone, and one of my children really needs me, that my date will be okay if I have to suddenly cancel once in a while. You'd think that other parents would automatically be fine with this, but I found this was not always the case. Don't assume that a person will understand just because he or she has children. Finally, do not be afraid to broach this subject with a potential partner, even one without children. He or she may be very understanding and supportive!

There is an obvious option that you may wish to consider as an alternative to breaking a date. Let's say your younger child has a stomach ache. If you're comfortable with the other person coming to your home with your children, suggest picking up some takeout food and a DVD. If the person you're dating doesn't understand this, DUMP THEM! And, turning the tables, they should dump you if you cannot, at some point, feel comfortable enough to go to their home with their kids if the occasion arises.

On the other hand, do not let your child or children rule your life, but that's another book. Balance is important.

Being a good parent may actually make you a more attractive partner. As funny as it may seem, I actually ended a relationship because I felt the person was, in my view, not there for her child when she needed her. When I looked to the future, I realized that if anything were to happen to me, I needed to feel confident that my children could turn to the person I was with to fulfill their needs and receive sound advice.

Second Commandment: Never Tolerate Lying in a Relationship

I remember one woman who constantly kept my stomach in knots. This was due to the fact that I was constantly being lied to. I noticed a number of small inconsistencies in her stories that in and of themselves didn't add up to a lot. She insisted that nothing was going on between her and her old (married) ex-boyfriend. When I confronted her with these inconsistencies, she told me that I was being ridiculous and worrying too much about the little things in life. Funny how all those little things added up to her lying!

Finally, about a year after I ended the relationship, she felt the need to cleanse her soul. She admitted to sleeping with the married ex-boyfriend while we were going out together. I learned to trust my gut. If I heard too many stories that simply did not make sense, or I caught someone in a series of small lies, I knew it was time to end the relationship.

Third Commandment: Avoid Those Who Are Self-Centered

I give a lot of myself to a relationship. I expect to be met halfway in return. That's why the essay in my profile defining a good relationship included the following: "A good relationship can only be built when each partner is willing to be open and meet the other person halfway."

What I did not discuss in my profile was consideration. A major key in developing and sustaining any relationship is that you must be considerate of the other person's feelings. By definition, self-centered people are not considerate of other people's needs and feelings, only their own.

I've dated two women whom I will call selfish. They were self-centered and inconsiderate with regard to my feelings. I'm also certain they would strongly disagree with this, but they aren't the ones who were on the receiving end. Also, I'm the one writing this book! They can go write their own book if they don't like what I have to say! I won't go into all of the details, but I will present three outtakes from these relationships to illustrate why this commandment is so essential.

One woman had a breathing disorder, so when I found that the air filter in her heating/air conditioning unit was not held firmly in place, I did two things. First, I vacuumed out all the air vents. Second, I purchased some materials, including a new air filter, at the local hardware store, and built a simple device to hold the filter in place. I spent nearly four hours on this project, and never received a simple thank you. I was told that people do things because they want to do them. Well, yes, I wanted to do it. But after I did, I got nada, nothing, zilch in return. A simple thank you would have gone a long way!

The other woman invited me and, later, my children to her beach club. It sounded like a nice offer, but each time we went, she ignored me 98% of the time we were there. We would always sit together with her sister and brother-in-law. The two sisters were so "into" what they had to say that they totally cut off all conversation with the brother-in-law and me for several hours at a time.

Later, she went on a two-week leisure trip to China on behalf of her mother's travel agency. Approximately one week into her trip, according to her itinerary she was supposed to be at a first class hotel in Beijing. So, I thought I would surprise her with a phone call. I wanted to let her know that I hoped she was having a great time and that I missed her. So, I let my fingers do the walking and I phoned China. It took several calls over a period of four hours before someone answered the phone in her room. When she finally answered the phone, she was extremely annoyed that I'd called her. All she could say, in a sarcastic tone, was that she couldn't believe I had called. She blew me off, saying she had to get off the phone. I apologized (though I'm not exactly sure why) and hung up.

Needless to say, I was very upset and disappointed. Later, when she returned home, she told me that I had interrupted the ambiance of her trip with my phone call. Can you believe that? With that, I dumped her. When anyone takes the time to call and ask me how things are, even if I feel they've interrupted me, I appreciate that they're thinking of me, and I let them know I appreciate it.

Fourth Commandment: Your Date Shall Be Communicative

This encompasses several different aspects of communication. For me, there is nothing like the give and take of a good verbal exchange! I hate it when attempting to have a conversation is like pulling teeth. You know what I mean. This problem can usually be detected when you first talk with someone on the phone ... but not always. There was one woman that I distinctly remember having had great phone conversations with, but for some reason when she was sitting there, right in front of me, she seemed incapable of carrying on the simplest of conversations.

When I am dating someone, I enjoy hearing her voice. This may sound crazy, but I truly do like hearing the voices of the people I care about. I enjoy not only hearing their voices but also knowing how their day is going, how their kids and family are. What's new? You know, I want to know the basic "yada yada yada" stuff.

I've dated several women who either just didn't have the time to talk (for some reason, they were often lawyers) or were just not very communicative. I know this can sometimes be a problem for other people, too. One friend told me about a guy she was dating. They had a nice relationship when they were together, but when they were apart, there was no communication other than "so, what time should I pick you up on Saturday? You should be wearing such and such." That's a very easy way to manage a relationship… but it's just not very satisfying, at least not for me!

Now that you've learned these four simple commandments, commit them to memory and let them guide your dating life. You'll be glad you did. I certainly was!

8 More Personal Experiences

Perhaps a Long Walk Off a Short Pier

My Worst Meeting

My absolute, without a doubt, worst Interview Date occurred about six weeks following my Knight in Shining Armor Story (Chapter 4), but before I discovered Internet Dating sites. I was not quite at the *OCOCD* (Obsessive Compulsive Online Chatting Disorder) level yet. So, with both hands available, I went into my favorite chat room and began to check out some of the participants' profiles, at least those that sounded like female members. I found one to be particularly interesting and thought she might be the perfect fit for me. So immediately I kicked off the conversation with my digital wit by sending an Instant Message to her saying "hi."

Like I said, this particular woman seemed quite promising at first. We chatted online for a few hours. We exchanged pictures, and I definitely liked what I saw. She indicated through an Instant Message that she also liked what she saw. We exchanged phone numbers and continued to chat on the phone that evening for a few more hours. We generally laughed and had a good time talking. So, after about three weeks of online chatting and phone calls, we decided it was time to meet.

She lived about 2.5 hours away, without traffic. The route between our homes traversed highways that were exceptionally congested during the week. Therefore, we decided to meet for an early Sunday morning brunch before the traffic picked up.

Fortunately (or unfortunately), I'd already acquired the knowledge necessary to make my way to her home town. This was because I'd recently visited the outskirts of her town in the middle of the night. She just happened to live in the same town where I earned my Knight in Shining Armor status. I was confident that it would be impossible for lightening to strike twice in the same city.

As we were planning our meeting, the woman broke the first rule of Internet Dating: she provided me with her home address. Again, let me state that while most people are normal and would never hurt a fly, you must get to know someone before you ever give out your address. Remember, even giving out your home phone number can be the same as giving out your address, and if you have a published phone number, there are many Internet websites that will perform a reverse lookup. As I've said before, cell phones are by far the safest way to initially talk.

I ignored that first broken rule, and looked forward to our meeting. On the appointed Sunday, I left home early on what I thought would be a great day for finding love.

Without having to face a lot of traffic, I arrived at the appropriate exit off the Southern State Parkway in just under two hours. As I wound my way through her town, I called to let her know that I was almost at her house. She told me to make a left turn, then a right turn, and that she was in the last house on the left at the end of the street. She told me that she was just finishing getting ready, and that her 15-year-old daughter would answer the door.

After I realized that I was a little more than a mile from her home, I became increasingly excited. She lived in a very nice area by the water, or so it seemed. But suddenly, the landscape changed from picturesque to run down. As I approached her home, I saw what appeared to be several washing machines on her front lawn. Upon pulling into the driveway, I realized that not only were these objects indeed washing machines, they were rusted through and through.

I wondered, "What kind of person keeps rusted appliances on her front lawn, and exactly when was it that I had my last Tetanus shot?" To answer the latter question, I probably received my last Tetanus shot when I was about 10 years old and cut myself while playing with some rusted appliances that my friends and I discovered in the backyard of an abandoned house. As far as the former question, I came up with three distinct possibilities:

1. She operated a salvage yard as a side business.

2. She was an artist that worked with rusty appliances, and was currently in her washing machine period.

3. She was a slob, and was well on the way to developing her own private shanty town.

Against my better judgment, meaning I should have immediately turned the car around and put the pedal to the (non-rusted) metal, I parked the car. With an apprehensive glance toward the rusted appliances, I killed the ignition, exited the car, marched forward and rang the doorbell.

I waited at the front door for what seemed like an eternity. Finally, after standing there for several minutes, I realized that the doorbell was out of order (probably rusted), so I knocked... gently. I certainly didn't want to discover that the door hinges were rusted like the outdoor appliances. If that was indeed the case, a strong knock could cause her front door to come crashing down and slam into her Ming dynasty vase that was possibly displayed just inside the front door.

Anyway, the woman's 15-year-old daughter appeared – a cigarette dangling from her lips, wearing a T-shirt featuring an obscene phrase. At that moment, I really wished I could have simply turned and run, but I heard footsteps descending the staircase. Not just the light steps of a lady, but the "clunk, clunk" of something else. I thought maybe this was her older son who played football, but no, Kemosabe, it was my date.

I was in shock. First of all she didn't look anything like her picture. Well, maybe if she'd lost 50 pounds and shaved 10 years from her age. Secondly, she was dressed in worn overalls, looking as if she was either going to:

1. Slop the pigs, or

2. Work on her rusted art sculptures.

On the lighter side of this "meeting of two lovers" fiasco ... that is, if you can imagine that a lighter side existed, there was the moment I realized that the door didn't come crashing down into what turned out to be a pile of worn out shoes and not the Ming dynasty vase!

Well, my jaw must have dropped to the floor, because she said "So, I guess I'm not what you expected."

I replied, "No, it was... just... seeing you... for the first time." I try never say anything rude to anyone I meet. I believe it's better to bite your tongue, keep your true feelings to yourself and say something nice. After all, (with any luck) you'll never see the person again.

Since I'm a man of my word, I suggested we immediately go out to breakfast just as soon as possible. I reminded her that I'd woken up early and was very hungry. Silently, I reasoned that no one in their right mind would be going to a restaurant this early on a Sunday morning. So, if we left right away, we (I) would not have to endure a long wait for a table and I could get through this nightmare as quickly and painlessly as possible.

We went upstairs to the main living area of the home, since we needed the yellow pages in order to find a restaurant that opened early (so I could get the heck out of there). If only I'd had this book to guide me! Let me draw a picture of her home for you. Paint was peeling all over the house. Dishes were piled high in the kitchen sink. Dirty pots and pans cluttered the stove. Junk was thrown all over the house. A mountain of newspapers covered the love seat. My date had to move piles of dirty laundry from the couch to make room for me to sit. You can just imagine what I was thinking to myself as I took it all in. Then it hit me! Of the three possible scenarios for her front yard display of appliances, I revoltingly came to the realization that she was indeed creating her very own private shanty town. In addition, I came to the regrettable conclusion that lightening can strike the same person twice in the same town.

Once again I told my date that I was very hungry and thought we should find a place that was already open for breakfast. After several phone calls, she located a nearby restaurant that was just opening for brunch.

I flew down the stairs, opened the door and took a deep breath of the fresh, though rusty ocean air. I started the car, layered on the hand sanitizer and waited for her to come out. I was in the middle of considering just how the heck I had gotten myself into this mess when she opened the car door and heaved herself in. We then set off on our way to the brunch buffet as my car listed toward the passenger (or since we were near the ocean, the starboard) side.

I can't remember if we talked much along the way, since I was too busy mentally kicking myself for having gotten into such a horrible situation. When we arrived at the restaurant, I dropped her off at the entrance and she went inside as I parked. There were only two other cars in the parking lot, and I took that as a good sign. This is unusual, since I usually take an empty restaurant parking lot as a bad sign, but the prospect of a short line versus good food was an easy choice. Since the restaurant was in a marina, I momentarily contemplated driving the car into the ocean and drowning myself.

As I entered the restaurant, I saw that she had already found her way to the buffet line. The hostess must have been expecting me, and escorted me to our booth. Once again, I briefly toyed with the idea of walking out the back door and drowning myself. Somewhat regrettably, I chose instead to have some breakfast, and I headed toward the buffet line.

My date was already on her way back to the table. I noticed that her plate contained more Eggs Benedicts than could easily fit – probably a dozen of them. I made my way to the buffet and selected two of the Eggs Benedict and some corned beef hash. Okay, I know I should have left out the corned beef hash and chosen something healthier, but I'm not perfect when it comes to eating. With my breakfast in hand, I returned to "our" table.

As I arrived, I noticed she was already devouring her food. In fact, she was now eating and talking with her mouth full. I was totally grossed out.

Then she summoned the waitress and asked if she could possibly have some more hollandaise sauce for her Eggs Benedict. There were probably five of them left, and she showed no signs of slowing down. The waitress came with one of those silver gravy boats full of the sauce. My date started to pour it over the eggs, slowly pivoting the gravy boat around its axis until it was fully rotated so she wouldn't miss out on a single drop. I've never seen anything quite like it.

I ate the entire meal with my head down, just looking at my plate. Even when my date went back for her second and third helpings, I just kept looking down. While I really wanted to have at least some sort of conversation, the only two subjects that came to mind were drowning and appliances, so I remained quiet. Finally, thankfully, we finished our meal and drove back to her home.

I got out of the car and walked her dutifully to the door. Then I announced I was leaving. I said I had eaten too much and wasn't feeling well. When we said our good-byes, she came at me attempting to give me a kiss. However, just in the nick of time, I pivoted my head almost as quickly as she pivoted the gravy boat, gave her a hug, and made the fastest possible retreat with my proverbial tail between my legs.

Marcia's Experiences

After 22 years of marriage, even the thought of starting to date was not appealing to me. Suddenly divorced, even though it was my choice, I was now a single mother with two sons. One was still in middle school and the other was heading off to college. I had spent the last 23 years with the same man, raising two boys and holding down a very demanding full-time job. So for me to start dating again was very much a foreign concept. Where or how was I going to meet eligible men, much less find the time and energy it would take to actually date? You know…re-learning the art of verbal dating banter and flirting, boning up on current events for intelligent conversation, fine tuning the wardrobe, etc. But at that point in my life, I couldn't think only about myself. I was responsible for ensuring that my two sons would survive and thrive through the divorce transition.

So, I chose to wait a while and work on not only making sure the boys were okay, but also working on getting back to being myself… a person I felt I had lost along the way. I was always told that I was a really fun and outgoing person. However, at the time of my divorce, I wasn't feeling that way at all and I realized that I hadn't felt that way for a very long time. In addition, I have to admit that, after 22 years of marriage, I enjoyed my "singleness." My younger son had a very active sports and social life. When I wasn't attending one of his numerous basketball games, I set aside time to enjoy doing the things that I wanted to do. But, let's face it; after a while it gets lonely and the thought of sharing time with a contemporary of the opposite sex did seem tempting.

I found myself in a quandary about reentering the dating scene. For me the question was "how do I get back into dating?" Going out to bars was not an option. Matchmaking services seemed weird. A few of my friends wanted to fix me up with their friends and relatives. I knew of a singles group that existed in my area, and I, of course, had heard all about Internet Dating. I spoke with friends who suggested that I would be more successful if I went the Internet route. While checking my email one evening, I decided that, just for fun, I would take a look at some of the Internet Dating sites. Within a few minutes I was searching for "potential" men in my area.

I found "looking" to be a lot of fun, but when it came down to signing up and actually trying it, I found myself making excuses for finding the time, taking and uploading pictures, etc. In reality, I was afraid to put myself out there. What if no one contacted me? What if no one responded to my profile? What if all of the men who did respond to my profile were losers? The hard cold truth hit me! I had lost the confidence that I had when I was dating in my teens and twenties. Could I meet new people, and would they find me worthy? So I took a rather radical approach, not one that might be right for others but one that ended up being perfect for me.

While searching the Internet site that ultimately led me to Jon, I noticed that the site offered "singles" vacations. Coming up was a four-night "singles" cruise. Wow! Since I love to cruise, and the cruise was departing from my area, was reasonably priced, and was over a holiday weekend, I thought "why not?" I immediately called two of my closest single girlfriends to tell them all of the reasons why we should take a chance and book this trip. Despite my best efforts, neither of them wanted to go. Well, that's not completely true. I believe that one of them really, really wanted to go on the cruise with me, but was even more afraid than I was. She initially seemed very interested, but then came up with several excuses why she couldn't go. Later that day, while speaking with my parents on the phone, I mentioned the cruise. My father (at age 80) was so positive (he must have called me 40 times that day encouraging me to go on the cruise) that I called the company for details. They assured me that:

1. There would be others my age, and

2. They would match me up with a roommate of the same sex and age group.

As nervous as I was, I made the decision to do it (of course, my father called me 4,000 more times that day expounding on all of the reasons why I should go. Could he have been worried about me becoming a reborn old maid?). I figured I had nothing to lose, so I booked it.

For the next four weeks I was continuously questioning my decision. "What have I done? What have I done?" Finally, the day arrived. I was so nervous. The previous day (okay, every day for the previous week), I packed, unpacked, packed, unpacked and packed my suitcase until the zipper on the case threatened to go on strike. I think you get the picture. Anyway, back to the big day that was going to put me back in the dating arena: I arrived at the pier, checked in, and headed to my cabin.

My unknown and unnamed roommate had already arrived and selected her side of the cabin, unpacked and obviously headed for greener pastures prior to my arrival. So I wandered around the ship for a while, and when I returned to the cabin to get ready for dinner, she was there waiting for me. What a relief it was to find that she was my age and appeared to be very nice. I had not been matched up with an axe murderer, which was a very good sign. We briefly exchanged backgrounds, got dressed and headed for the first of many planned "mix and mingle" events to be held over the course of the cruise. I had a blast. I mingled. I mixed. I made friends. I had two men flirting with me. It was a great ego booster. It was just what the doctor ordered! The funny thing is that I would have been just as fine entering the world of Internet Dating without the cruise. I just didn't realize it at the time.

So when I returned from the trip, I began working on my profile in earnest. I didn't rush it because I wanted to do my best to portray myself to others in a down-to-earth, accurate, yet entertaining way.

My First Date

So, I finally finished my profile, sent in the picture and waited for my profile and picture to be approved and posted on the Internet Dating site. Up it came, and now the waiting began: wait, wait, wait. Please let someone respond, I thought. Lo and behold, I received an email the very next day. He seemed nice. Asked a lot of questions – where I went to school, etc. I looked at his profile. He said he was fit and trim, liked the water and owned a boat, had a fun personality, etc. We exchanged several emails and agreed to meet after work for a drink at a waterfront restaurant. I purposely scheduled the meeting between work and a 6:00 PM meeting I had to attend. I arrived at the restaurant and I started to check out the place to see if he was already there. I arrived first, apparently. I made a dash for the restroom to check my hair and lipstick. When I returned, a man approached me and I realized that it was him.

Well, I have to tell you, he wasn't exactly "as advertised." He was a good three to four inches shorter than he stated in his profile, and if he fell overboard from his boat, he would have been okay, since he had what appeared to be an inner tube under his shirt to keep him afloat. We sat down and ordered a drink. Wait a minute: was that his real hair or a toupee? I kept trying to sneak a closer look without him noticing, but I didn't want to stare, so I gave up trying to figure it out. He was actually very nice, but I just couldn't get a good rapport going with him. After about 45 minutes of small talk, I was running out of things to say. Just in the nick of time, he asked if I wanted to see his boat. Thank goodness: anything to break the monotony!

So we walked over to the boat slips and there among the big 30 and 40 foot boats was the boat he had bragged about numerous times. Now, I'm not one of those people impressed by lots of money, big boats, houses, etc., but I have to tell you it was pretty funny. He made it sound like he owned a small yacht, but it was just a regular 18-foot fishing boat. Nice, well maintained, gets the job done, and certainly 18 feet more boat than I owned, but as I learned along the way: be who you are and don't pretend to be someone that you aren't. He really wanted to be something he wasn't, and I think that bothered me the most. Would I have thought less of him if he said that he was a little overweight and a little shorter? I don't think so. Would I have still met him? The short answer is: probably.

Back-To-Back Dates

I must admit to corresponding with several men at one time. I did actually have three different dates within a four-day period. What was I thinking? The first date was for lunch with a gentleman relocating to South Florida from New York. He was a doctor, but was not currently practicing because he said "he didn't like it anymore," whatever that means. We met at a very exclusive restaurant in Coral Gables for lunch. He said on his profile that he was 6' 4" (I'm 5'), and guess what? He didn't lie. We had a nice lunch, which consisted of him talking about himself and his two ex-wives 95% of the time and his mother 4% of the time, which left about 1% to speak about the weather. I don't think he once asked me a question. The food was great, though. As we left the restaurant and walked to the street, I began to thank him for the lovely lunch and tell him goodbye. All of a sudden he left his stratosphere, bent down, grabbed me and kissed me with a rather sloppy French kiss. I laughed all the way home. He called several times after that, but I never agreed to see him for a second date.

The following day, I had lunch with an executive who worked for one of the major travel-related companies in my area. Of course, this was appealing to me because, as I mentioned earlier, I love to travel. I had such high hopes. This was the one occasion I let a man pick me up at my house without knowing him. Let me stress: do not do this! I was lucky, and didn't have any problems, but I shouldn't have done it. I guess I figured, given his background and where he worked, it would be okay. Without really knowing him, however, I should have realized that any or all of his profile and subsequent conversations could have been lies. It was a lapse in judgment on my part. Anyway, the weather was not cooperating. It was pouring, so he called me to come out when he arrived at my home. That was his first mistake. Then he took me to a restaurant/bar/pool hall for lunch, saying it was his favorite place for hamburgers. I love a good hamburger, but this was a pretty sleazy place, definitely not a prime first-date location. That was his second mistake. With regard to his appearance and personality, he was short, had thinning hair, was nicely built and attractive, but he had short arms. I know it sounds strange, but they seemed out of proportion to the rest of his body, sort of like a human T-Rex. I know it was wrong, but I could not help but focus my attention on his arms.

He was talkative, but (again) like the previous day's date, this man preferred to do all of the talking. And, of course, he spoke about his favorite subject: himself. That was his third and final mistake! Anyway, two hours later, and still listening to how he prefers tall blondes (by the way, I'm short and brunette, which was obvious from my profile) and that his second wife was tall and blonde, I was fortunate enough to have my cell phone ring and "oops, I have to go" put a merciful end to this date. Well, not exactly the end of the date, because now I had to share a 30-minute car ride back to my home. (Hope you paid attention to Jon's Meeting Rule #2: Don't be picked up at your house.) Anyway, I figured out how to make the ride home as painless as possible. I asked him something about himself. Then, I just sat back and pretended to listen.

Two days later, I went out on my third date. He was younger by seven years, never married, and seemed like he would be great fun. We exchanged a few funny emails and phone conversations, and decided to meet for happy hour near my work. I walked in, and he was at the bar. You could tell just by looking at him that he would be an entertaining kind of guy. Let me also add that he was a "biker," by night and on weekends, and a Yuppie by day, since he drove a foreign sports car to work. I knew I would never get on the back of a motorcycle again at this point in my life, so the relationship was doomed before it ever began. We had a great time together that afternoon, but we both knew we were not destined to be with each other. Talk about being at different stages in life! He wanted to get married and have babies. I wanted my two "babies" to graduate college, get married and have their own babies! :) I'm looking forward to spoiling my grandkids.

My Rebound

My first real relationship via Internet Dating lasted about six months. I emailed him first; an email volley ensued, followed by several phone calls, which finally resulted in our meeting. We met in the bar of a popular restaurant, and things went so well that we progressed to dinner. His good points were that he was smart, had a good job, maintained a good relationship with his two daughters, whose ages were similar to my sons', and he seemed to enjoy nice places and things. On the negative side, he was somewhat aloof, drank a little too much, and would sometimes drop off the radar for several days at a time. This was particularly disconcerting to me when, without notice, there were suddenly no calls, especially since he always (except during these episodes) called every night.

He also expected me to be available at his whim. For example, he would sometimes call at the last minute and expect me to be available to get together. He would usually prefer that I meet him or go to his place, since that was obviously easier for him.

Remember Jon speaking of the "Bad Boy" type? In thinking about it, he fit the description with a capital T that rhymes with B that stands for bad... as in "Bad Boys." But for the transitional or rebound relationship, he actually was very good for me. I recognized that serious relationships involve two people who care about each other, and attempting a relationship with a self-centered person was not for me. Been there, done that.

Fixed Up By A Friend... Some Friend!

I had one experience where I was fixed up by a friend who thought his cousin and I would be a perfect match.

Perfect? No, but he was (is) a really nice guy that I dated sporadically until I met Jon. Even though we were about the same age (okay, I was a couple of years older), he had one daughter who was seven years old and stayed with him two afternoons a week, every other weekend and the entire summer.

Needless to say, his priority was thankfully in the right place (with his daughter), so we basically enjoyed each other's company when it fit into the schedule. We continued to speak from time to time, and when Jon and I became engaged, he wished me well, telling me that he wasn't surprised because "all of the good ones get snapped up quickly!" Truly one of the nicest of compliments anyone could ever receive.

9 It's Up to You!

The world can be delivered to your door; what you do with it depends on you.

What Stigma?

Today, Internet Dating is popular and widely accepted as a route for meeting members of the opposite (or same for that matter) sex, whether your goal is friendship and companionship or marriage and children. Although there was a time when some people viewed Internet sites as the electronic equivalent of personal ads, which (in their view) were only used by lovelorn desperados, the unattractive or those suffering from peculiar "problems," that viewpoint is now as antiquated as a rotary phone.

Most people turn to Internet Dating for one of two reasons (or both):

1. ***There's no viable alternative.*** Especially for those of us over 35, the traditional "dating wells" have dried up or the "waters" have turned a bit brackish. We're no longer surrounded by hundreds of eligible people as we were in high school or college. Our friends *TG* (Thank God) know few singles that would make a good match for us. We don't throw parties every weekend and we may not work for a large corporation, etc.

2. ***It's fun and exciting.*** At least in the beginning, the possibilities for meeting the right person can seem almost endless. After all, I have read where there are over 50 million individuals signed up on various Internet Dating sites, looking for someone! You're no longer limited to dating people you meet by chance, or who are within your current social network. You can constantly chat with new people, set up Interview Dates, and look forward to spending countless "nights on the town," instead of time alone in your home. Internet Dating is a fun and challenging quest for love, and most people enjoy the challenge.

It's up to you to decide whether you want to take the chance. Nobody, including me, is recommending that you launch an Internet Dating career if it doesn't seem right for you. And I'd never suggest that you take the plunge if you're not ready. If you're still getting over a long-term relationship or marriage that went south, it is my belief that nothing cures a bad relationship like a good one. My advice, if you feel you are ready, is to get out there and grab some of those transitional dating experiences.

Dealing with Rejection

If you haven't dated in a long time, your biggest challenge may be learning how to gracefully accept rejection. It's important to learn to accept rejection without taking it personally. It's also important to learn how to gently let other people down if they're not right for you. For many of us, it's nearly impossible not to take rejection personally, but here are a few tips that (at a minimum) should help soften the blow.

If you receive no response, or a rejection, to your initial email:

- If your "target" is a new website member (especially an attractive one), he or she may have been flooded with emails within hours of posting a profile. If you've received no reply, or what appears to be a form rejection email, email the person at a later date. By this point, the "grand opening rush" will have died down, and, if the person isn't seriously involved with someone else, a personalized follow-up might spark some interest.

- If the "target" is not a new member, assume a "job search" mentality. If you do not receive a reply to your initial email of interest, then take the attitude that this person has done you a favor because:

    a. The position has been filled, or

    b. The job wasn't right for you.

- Please keep in mind that you will (or already have) rejected applicants, too. Everybody gets their turn to be on the receiving end of a rejection.

If you are consistently rejected during the initial contact phase then:

- Ask a trusted friend or colleague to review your profile and a sampling of the emails you've sent. It's possible that your profile simply does not stand out, or that you're saying something that turns people off. I'm not suggesting there's anything wrong with you, but since most people aren't masters of the written word, it's always a good idea to have a friend review what you have written. It's also entirely possible that you're not communicating as effectively as you could.

  Some may feel that you might possibly be misrepresenting yourself when there appears to be a conflict between your words and your pictures, or simply between the pictures themselves. What I'm saying is that it's a problem if one or more of your pictures appear to have been taken years (or decades) before what appear to be the current ones.

- Post a photo. I don't care how unattractive you *think* you are: you won't receive many responses if prospects can't see what you look like. Chances are that:

  a. You're more attractive than you think, and

b. Some people will find you attractive, unless (to be honest) you're seeking someone well out of your "looks league."

I'm really not trying to be cruel, but if you're just average looking, and you insist on contacting only people with "supermodel good looks," you've got an uphill climb ahead. Try the mass marketing approach.

- Post a different photo. Plenty of people think they look great in particular photos, but if they were to ask their friends they might receive a different opinion. Therefore, ask your best friends what they think of the photos you've posted and take their advice (to a point) if they suggest substituting different pictures.

If you are consistently being rejected during the Interview phase then:

- Assume a "job search mentality." Okay, so you made it past the resume and telephone interview phases, but as it turned out, the job wasn't right for you. It's time to look for a better opportunity.

- Ask, "Am I targeting the right people, or am I targeting (or responding to) the types of people I've been with before or who've rejected me before." Some people stick with "the devil they know" instead of leaving their comfort zones to find people who might be right for them.

- Your posted photo may be "deceptive." I'm not saying you intentionally tried to mislead, but maybe that "best picture ever taken" isn't the one you should run with. No, you don't want to upload an unflattering picture either, but at the same time, your "best picture ever taken" may deserve that status because of some unusual quirk of lighting, camera angle, etc. Again, ask trusted friends and relatives to suggest photos that are both flattering and representative of how you look today.

- Also ask trusted friends, relatives and colleagues about the following:

  a. Do I dress for success? At the one extreme are the people who dress the way they did during their youth, people who freeze their appearance in time, as if they were the picture of Dorian Gray (they get older but their hairstyle and clothing stays the same) or they try to dress in a style that is not age appropriate. I've "interviewed" several women who were in their late 40s and showed up for the date dressed like their 18-year-old daughters. Ladies – please do NOT borrow your daughter's clothing!

     Even if you have the greatest body known to mankind, please be realistic and dress your age. You don't have to dress dowdy either: just leave the bare-belly-pierced midriff for another time. At the other end of the spectrum are people who stop caring about their appearance entirely. People, it's one thing to wear what's comfortable, but this is an interview! Put your best foot forward.

b. "What did I say?" It's possible that red flags are sprouting from your head whenever you go on an Interview Date. This may stem from nerves, baggage from previous relationships, or simply because you may not have dated in a decade or two. Replay your latest date conversation with members of your "support team" to determine if you're scaring people off.

c. Annoying habits! Who me? The sister of a friend who was having trouble moving past the first date, finally told him that he had "more ticks than a five-dollar watch." When she pointed out that he constantly fiddled with his hair and mustache, and tried too hard to be funny, he gradually learned to relax. He also learned to listen and ask questions of his dates, which proved to be an extremely effective strategy.

Dignity, Always Dignity

If and when you are rejected, please accept it with grace and dignity.

Imagine that a television crew is videotaping your Internet Dating experiences for a new reality show. At the end of the evening, would you prefer that millions of viewers see you shaking hands with your date and wishing them the best of luck, or would you prefer the audience watch you screaming expletives and being handcuffed by the cops as you try to throw rocks through their window?

If you made the mistake of conducting your Initial Interview Date over dinner, and your date is rolling her eyes and checking her watch every 30 seconds, suggest near the conclusion of the meal that it's time for both of you to head home, and thank the person for a pleasant evening. Sure, you could point out the eye-rolling and watch-checking to score some face-saving points, but will that really accomplish anything? The kind of person who exhibits rude behavior isn't likely to listen to you anyway. Remember to keep the Initial Interview Dates short.

Conversely, when YOU are the person doing the rejecting, consider adapting the "no thank you" templates I provided in Chapter 3. And, if you're on an Interview Date, do your best to (at least) feign interest in what the other person is saying until the end of the interview. Then, tell the other person that you had a nice time and leave it at that. Sayonara, Baby!

In most cases, your date will either feel the same way that you do, or will understand that there won't be a second date, even if they wished there could be.

Whatever you do, DON'T (in no particular order):

- Tell them you'll call!

- Give them a passionate good night kiss!

- Recite a laundry list of why you think things won't work out, even if you're asked!

- Insult them!

- Agree to another date!

- Sleep with them out of pity or any other reason, including alcohol! Don't forget the dangers of MUI.

ABOVE ALL, feel free to disregard any or all of my advice if you think the situation warrants it. I may have written a book, but I don't know it all. There are times when little white lies are appropriate to spare another person's feelings. What's more, romantic relationships are so varied and complex that there are exceptions to every rule, however well-intentioned the rule may be.

Ultimately, Internet Dating sites simply offer a new and better tool for getting you out there to meet the potential love of your life. Beyond that, dating is dating, and your love life is your own. It's up to you how to proceed. Good Luck!

10 Poetry for Internet Daters

At the touch of love
everyone becomes a poet.
- Plato

Who says the Internet can't be just as romantic as real life? Maybe electronic roses aren't quite as nice as the real thing, but when it comes to the language of love, online romantic e-cards or emails can be a wonderful prelude to being together in person. And, of course, when you have a broken heart or your love life is getting you down, Internet Daters sometimes turn to poetry to declare their feelings – in the same way real-life Romeos express theirs. Here's my attempt, though admittedly not a very good one, at writing Internet Dating poetry! I wrote it for a female friend describing her experiences.

Bits and Bytes of Desire

Bits and bytes flowing through the Internet
My heart and desires are turned into zeros and ones
My soul is poured into a profile
I am slightly uncertain as

My picture is up there for all to scrutinize.

As I search for my love
Men around the world are searching for me

I sift through my email
I check out their profiles
I consider for a moment
Am I simply flypaper for pathetic men?

I finally write an initial letter
Then I write two
Three, four and five follow
Nothing in return

But wait a minute
There is something in my inbox
I have been waiting an eternity
He was away
He was my letter number one

We email back and forth
We talk for hours
We are the love of each other's lives
We decide to meet

I drive there
He is on his way
I wait in anticipation
He walks in
My heart sinks

I am now waiting for letter number two.

-*The End*

11 The "How To" Chapter

All Systems are Go!

Now that you have all the background information, including my warnings and guidelines, let's put the entire process together from start to finish.

Step 1: Deciding Which Sites To Use

There are a slew of Internet Dating sites out there. Most let you post your information for free. However, most also require that you purchase a subscription if you wish to initiate contact with or respond to another member, or simply read the emails others have sent you. As to which one is right for you, only you can be the judge of that. There are literally thousand of sites to choose from that cater to just about everything or everyone imaginable. Ask some of your friends for suggestions or simply search the web for the site that best suits you. I was a member of three different sites at various times during my six-year quest.

Until you find the site(s) you want to use, I have created a web site for you to start on. The site is located on the Internet at http://www.gr8mates.com and while this is a fully functional site, it is not our intent for you to use this site alone for placing or perusing potential candidates. It was created for demonstration purposes only. If you happen to be one of the first ones on the site, don't worry. With everyone hopefully buying this book (one must be optimistic to try Internet Dating, let alone write about it), there should be many people to view. The site is useful for learning how to set up your profile on a typical Internet Dating site. Take advantage of it while it's free!

Step 2: Peruse the Site

You don't have to be a member to view the profiles and pictures on gr8mates.com. This lets you peruse the site at your leisure before deciding whether to become a member. To look it over, simply type http://www.gr8mates.com into your computer's browser. Then, once you are at the home page, type in the parameters for the kind of person you wish to search for. The results will then appear.

It will make this chapter easier to understand and more enjoyable if you follow along on your own computer. So take this guide and go online to give it a try.

After you have typed in http://www.gr8mates.com, you will come to a page that looks like this:

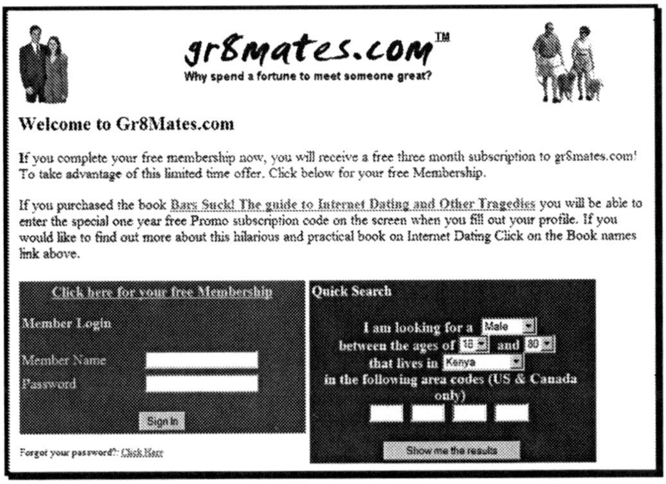

Figure 1

This is the site's home page – at least, this is how it looked at the time of writing of this book. It may be a little different by the time you arrive here, but the functionalities should be approximately the same.

Step 3: Perform a Quick Search

In the "Quick Search Box" shown above, enter/select the following information by selecting the appropriate items from the pull-down menus:

1. Male or female.
2. The age range you are looking for.
3. The country where potential dates should reside (if the country does not appear that means that there are no members in that country).
4. Area code (optional).

Once you've done this, click on "Show Me the Results."

Depending on your selections, you'll see the following screen with the results of your selection:

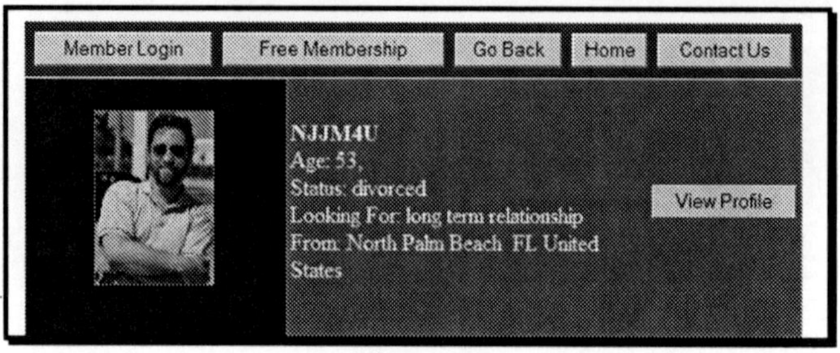

Figure 2

I found me! Yup, this was the profile I used on a different site to catch my own Internet Bride.

From here, you have several options. You may:

1. Click on the "View Profile Button" to see my entire profile.
2. Log in, if you are an existing member.
3. Choose to begin your Free Membership.
4. Return to the previous screen.
5. Go to the gr8mates.com home page.
6. Click on "Contact Us" and write us an email.

For our example, we will begin by choosing the first option and view the entire profile. This is what you will see:

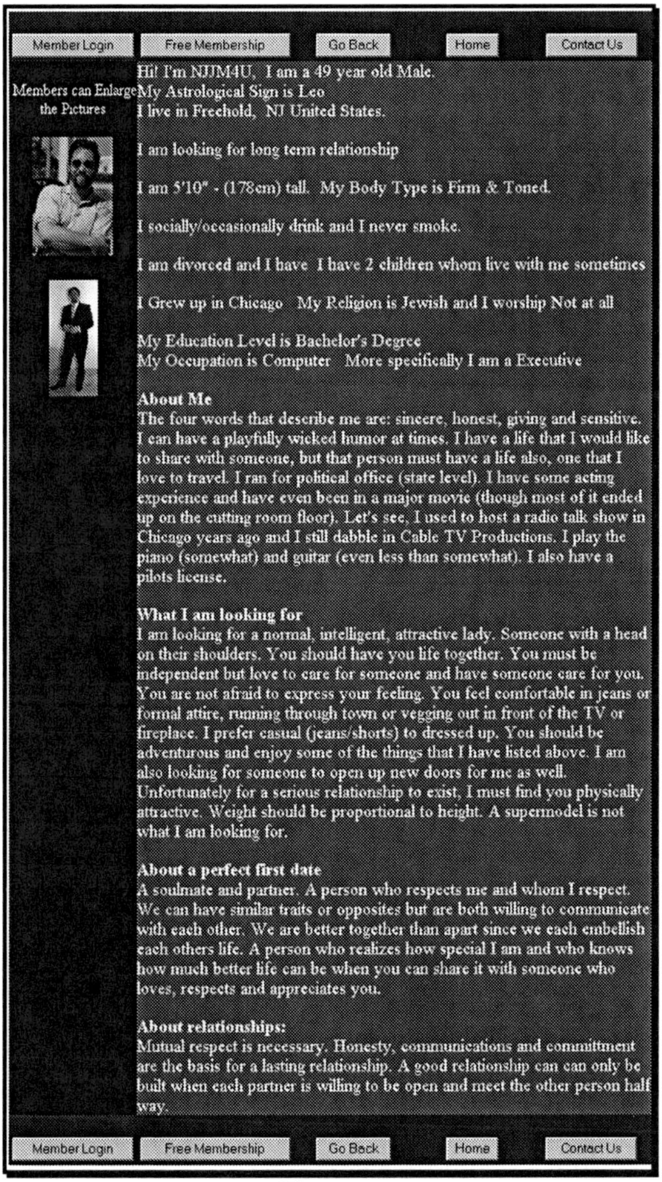

Member Login | Free Membership | Go Back | Home | Contact Us

Members can Enlarge the Pictures

Hi! I'm NJJM4U, I am a 49 year old Male.
My Astrological Sign is Leo
I live in Freehold, NJ United States.

I am looking for long term relationship

I am 5'10" - (178cm) tall. My Body Type is Firm & Toned.

I socially/occasionally drink and I never smoke.

I am divorced and I have I have 2 children whom live with me sometimes

I Grew up in Chicago My Religion is Jewish and I worship Not at all

My Education Level is Bachelor's Degree
My Occupation is Computer More specifically I am a Executive

About Me
The four words that describe me are: sincere, honest, giving and sensitive. I can have a playfully wicked humor at times. I have a life that I would like to share with someone, but that person must have a life also, one that I love to travel. I ran for political office (state level). I have some acting experience and have even been in a major movie (though most of it ended up on the cutting room floor). Let's see, I used to host a radio talk show in Chicago years ago and I still dabble in Cable TV Productions. I play the piano (somewhat) and guitar (even less than somewhat). I also have a pilots license.

What I am looking for
I am looking for a normal, intelligent, attractive lady. Someone with a head on their shoulders. You should have you life together. You must be independent but love to care for someone and have someone care for you. You are not afraid to express your feeling. You feel comfortable in jeans or formal attire, running through town or vegging out in front of the TV or fireplace. I prefer casual (jeans/shorts) to dressed up. You should be adventurous and enjoy some of the things that I have listed above. I am also looking for someone to open up new doors for me as well. Unfortunately for a serious relationship to exist, I must find you physically attractive. Weight should be proportional to height. A supermodel is not what I am looking for.

About a perfect first date
A soulmate and partner. A person who respects me and whom I respect. We can have similar traits or opposites but are both willing to communicate with each other. We are better together than apart since we each embellish each others life. A person who realizes how special I am and who knows how much better life can be when you can share it with someone who loves, respects and appreciates you.

About relationships:
Mutual respect is necessary. Honesty, communications and committment are the basis for a lasting relationship. A good relationship can can only be built when each partner is willing to be open and meet the other person half way.

Member Login | Free Membership | Go Back | Home | Contact Us

Figure 3

You will be able to scroll down and read through my entire profile. Once again, at the bottom of the screen, you will have a number of options from which to choose.

Step 4: Set Up a Profile

Now that you've gotten an idea of what this site has to offer, let's set up a Free Membership and create a profile. In order to do this, click on the "Free Membership" button. You will then be presented with a Disclaimer Screen, where the terms and conditions of membership are shown for either your acceptance or rejection. The following is just a snippet of the Membership Disclaimer (of course, you should read the entire website disclaimer carefully):

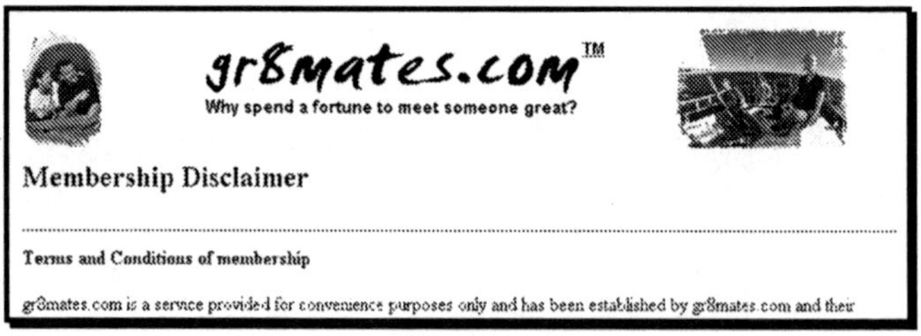

Figure 4

If you agree, click on the "Agree" button, and this will take you to the Membership questionnaire. If you do not agree, then click on the "Decline" button. This will take you back to the previous screen.

Assuming you read the disclaimer and agree with its terms, click on the "Agree" button so you can start filling in the New Membership Application. The application looks like this:

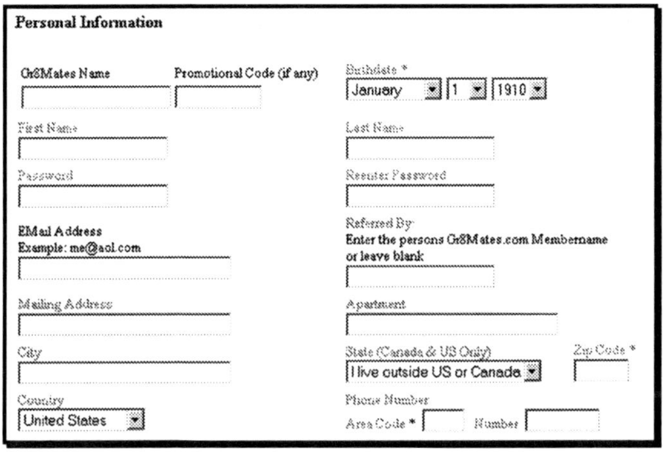

Figure 5

The first entry you will make on this form will be your Gr8Mates Name. This needs to be unique to you, so give it some thought. We suggest that you do not use your given name as part of your GR8Mates Name (for safety and security reasons). If you select a name that has already been chosen, you will receive a message after you click on the "Sign Me Up Now" button at the bottom of the page. If this happens, simply come up with a different name.

Next, in order to activate your trial subscription, type in **BarsSuck** in the Promotional Code space.

Note: for your safety, none of the information requested in red font will be made available to other members. Continue to fill out the rest of the form.

Be honest! As I stressed earlier, in my opinion, three of the most reprehensible lies involve your age, marital status and the number of children you have. This whole Internet Dating thing only works when we're all honest with each other. Trust me, I know!

Now you will need to select a password. Because of the way passwords work, if an error occurs, you will need to retype your password each time you are returned to this screen.

After you have entered all of your personal information, scroll down and continue to fill out the questionnaire.

This next set of questions, “About Me,” refers to specifics about you. This information is used to assist people searching gr8mates.com to either locate or eliminate a group of people from their searches.

Since this information is vital in a search, it’s crucial that you answer each question completely and honestly:

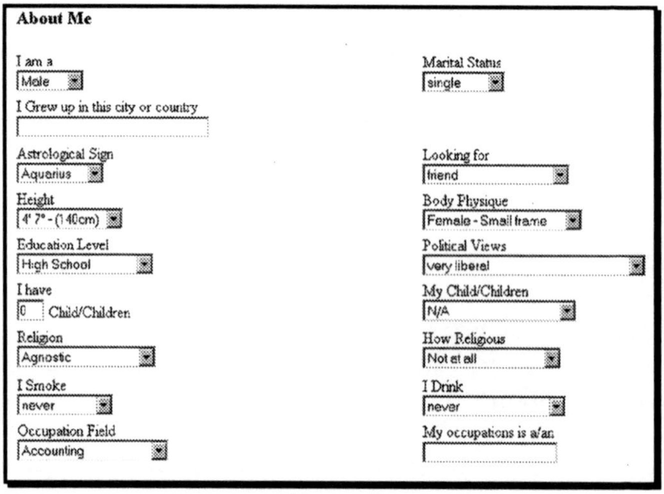

Figure 6

Select the appropriate answers from the pull-down menus provided. Enter the geographical area in which you grew up and your occupation.

Next is the "Essay" section. No, you're not going to be corrected or graded, but others will definitely judge you by how and what you write. In fact, this may be the third most important area when it comes to finding the right person (the first being gender and the second being your photos). People *do* read the essays. I cannot stress enough the importance of content, spelling and grammar. I have seen photos of very attractive women that I chose not to pursue thanks to their inability to write. While I was searching for an attractive lady, beauty was not my only criterion. I desired a lady who was as intelligent as she was attractive.

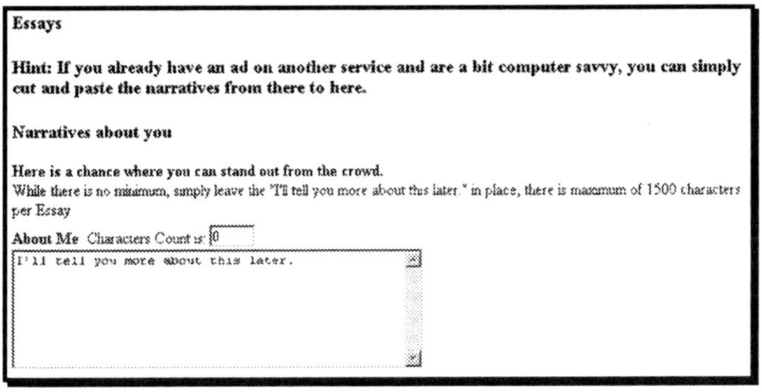

Figure 7

There are four different essays:

1. About Me (where you tell others what makes you special).
2. About the person I would like to meet.
3. What I like to do on a date.
4. What makes a good relationship.

Each essay can be as short as 50 characters or as long as 1,500 characters. You must enter a minimum of 50 characters before your membership will be accepted.

If you haven't read the section on essays in Chapter 3, please read it now. It is incredibly helpful, with many tips on how to develop a narrative. It also provides a sample essays to inspire you.

After you've completed the application and have double-checked the answers, click on the "Sign Me Up Now" Button:

Note: you may update any of your information at any time.

After you've clicked the "Sign Me Up Now" button, you will be brought to a screen where you may sign on. The Member Login screen looks like this:

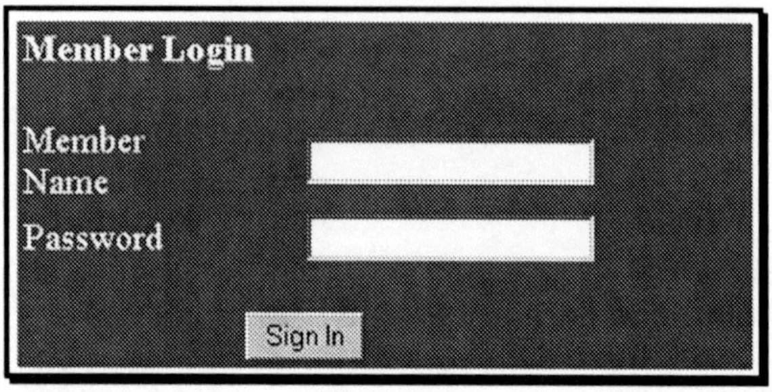

Figure 9

First, enter the Member Name you have chosen, followed by your password. Then click the "Sign In" Button.

Once you are signed on, you will have access to the entire membership area.

Step 5: Take a Look at the Members Menu

This is what the Members Menu looks like:

Figure 10

Let's take a closer look at the function of each option when selected.

Home

This button brings you back to this page.

View My Profile

This button allows you to view your profile the way others see it.

Look Up a Profile

This button allows you to view another member's profile.

Update My Profile

This button allows you to update your personal information.

Update My Essays

This button allows you to update your essays.

Manage Pictures

This button allows you to upload or delete pictures as well as to choose your primary picture. Pictures are only shown after they have been approved.

Subscriptions

This will allow you to either buy a one-year subscription or extend your current subscription by one year.

Favorites

This button will take you to an area where you can see all of those members that you have chosen to be your favorites.

Search

As a member, you can create a detailed member search and then save it for future use.

Contact Us

Use this button to send the folks at gr8mates.com an email.

Other Services

Here you can do things like change your password or delete your membership.

Logoff

This button signs you out of the system.

Step 6: Get Your Pictures Online

I've already said plenty about the importance of pictures (honest pictures) for promoting a successful Internet Dating career. With that said, let's get started uploading your pictures for others to see.

To upload a picture, begin by selecting the "Manage Picture" button from the Members Menu. This will take you to the "Manage Your Pictures" section:

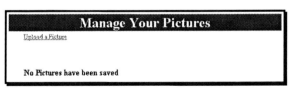

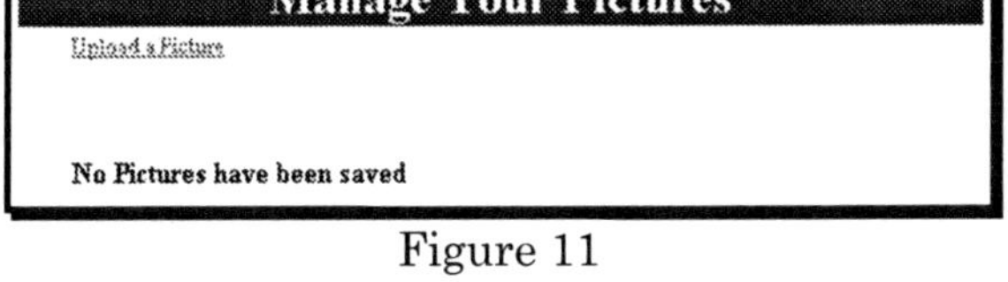

Figure 11

When you are ready to upload your picture, click on the "Upload a Picture" link.

Now you should see the following screen:

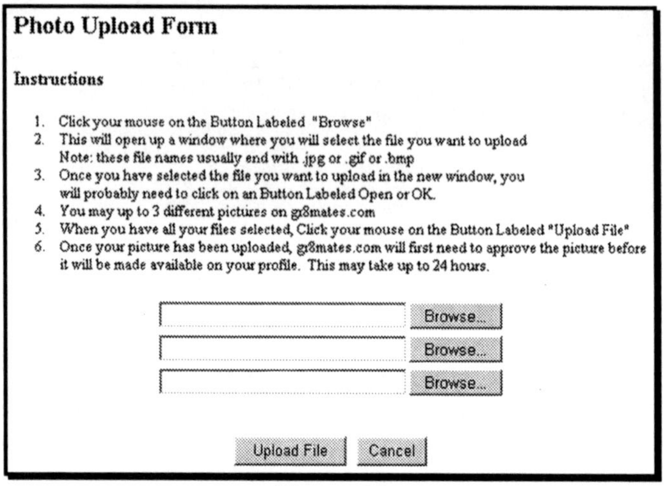

Photo Upload Form
Instructions
1. Click your mouse on the Button Labeled "Browse"
2. This will open up a window where you will select the file you want to upload
Note: these file names usually end with .jpg or .gif or .bmp
3. Once you have selected the file you want to upload in the new window, you will probably need to click on an Button Labeled Open or OK.
4. You may up to 3 different pictures on gr8mates.com
5. When you have all your files selected, Click your mouse on the Button Labeled "Upload File"
6. Once your picture has been uploaded, gr8mates.com will first need to approve the picture before it will be made available on your profile. This may take up to 24 hours.
Browse...
Browse...
Browse...
Upload File
Cancel

Figure 12

You may upload up to three different pictures as part of your Member Profile. To upload a picture, you must first have a scanned picture on your computer. It should be either a .jpg or a .bmp (these are just different types of picture files). The JPEG (jpg) format is preferable because they are smaller and faster to upload/download.

For this example, we will upload a picture named jon1.jpg. To begin, let's click on the top "Browse" button. In Windows, this brings up the following file selection box:

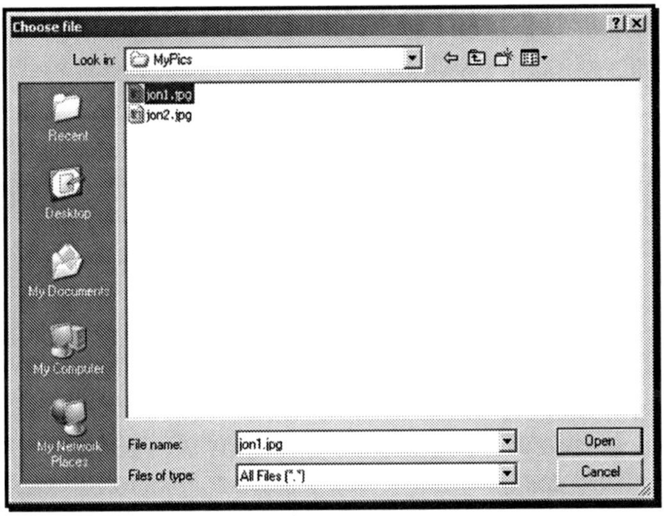

Figure 13

For demonstration purposes, we'll be selecting and uploading pictures from my computer. Select the jon1.jpg file and then click the "Open" button. This will fill in the blank area in front of the "Browse" button that we clicked on:

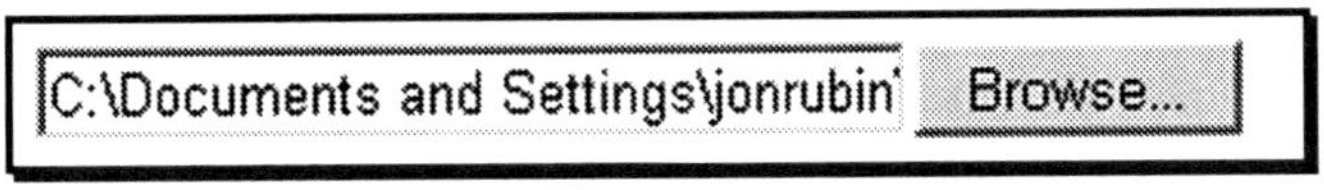

Figure 14

Now we will click on the "Upload File" button that is at the bottom of the screen, and voila, the following will appear:

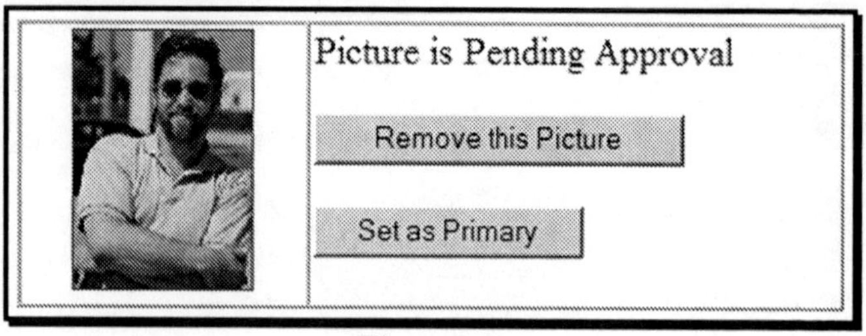

Figure 15

Pictures need to be approved to ensure that no one uploads any obscene or inappropriate material. It usually takes no more than 24 hours for a picture to be approved.

You may repeat the process until you have three pictures uploaded.

If you want to delete a picture, simply click on the "Remove This Picture" button. To make a picture your primary photo, that is, the picture that appears as a result of a search (see Figure 2, above), all you have to do is click on the "Set as Primary" button next to the picture of your choice.

Once your pictures have been approved, you can click on the "View My Profile" button on the Members Menu to see how others will see your profile.

Easy, right? Just a few simple, straightforward steps to get your profile set up and become a member of a thriving online site full of people just like you, looking for love on the Internet.

12 Epilogue

Simply Said...
Internet Dating Works!

During my six years of Internet Dating, I met many wonderful ladies. I probably talked (on the phone) with nearly 300 women and met approximately 150 of them. While the majority of the women I met were not right for me, I developed two relationships that each lasted a year and another that lasted six months. Ultimately, I met my bride through the Internet.

In the time during which my profile was online for others to see, I received between zero and 12 emails per day. Then, one fateful midsummer night, I received the very witty (as I've been told many a time) email that was going to change my love life for good. Here it is!

> *Hi. I really enjoyed your profile ... no moss growing under your feet (weak, I know)!! What do you consider long distance?*

At the time, I failed to immediately realize that this was THE email that was going to change my entire life. I didn't even respond right away, as I've continually been reminded! Well, as I always say, *patience is a virtue when it comes to Internet Dating.* So is persistence!

After several days (or more, according to Marcia), my correspondent, having been less than enamored with the lack of an immediate response from me, wrote me another less verbose, less witty email. Below is the entire content of the email:

Hi.

At that point, I knew that I'd write her back in the near future. Let me be honest: I liked her picture, and not only did I like what she had written in her profile, but I was intrigued by some of it. However, she lived almost two hours away! *OMG* (Oh My God), not another *GC* (Geographically Challenged) female!

In a twist of fate, I knew that in a month or so I would be moving closer to where this wonderful lady lived. I decided that I would definitely write her soon and that I was not going to blow her off.

A few days later, she IM'ed me, repeating the brilliance of her last email:

Hi.

I was on the phone with someone (probably someone else who had emailed me prior to her email) and responded by telling her,

"I'm on the phone right now.
Here's my real email address.......

Write me there."

I guess she decided that she would respond just about as quickly as I had responded to her initial email, i.e., she didn't!

Anyway, I felt bad and so, when I saw her online a few days later, I immediately decided to Instant Message (IM) her. I apologized for being on the phone when she had first tried to IM me. I said that I really wanted to talk with her. We IM'ed for a few minutes, and then, deciding she might well be worth pursuing, I asked for and received her cell phone number. No, I didn't forget to use the *67 before I called, just in case she was the Texas Chainsaw Lady. (Subtle joke there, since she's from Texas.) It turned out that she had to pick up some friends at the airport later that day, which was halfway between us, so we agreed to meet there and have a drink.

We also agreed to take our cell phones with us to the airport to decide where to meet once we arrived. But since cell phone coverage is not always perfect (kind of like Internet Dating!), I always have plan "B" ready. I told her I would be at the entryway to the check-in counter for a particular airline at 2:30. As usual, I arrived about 15 minutes early. I scoped out the bar and then found my way to the airline counter. I was now at our established public meeting place 10 minutes early.

I kept waiting...and waiting...and waiting... It was now 2:30 and there was no sign of her. I tried her cell phone, but there was no answer, only her voice mail.

At 2:37, I tried her phone again, with the same result...nothing! There was still no sign of her. More waiting...and waiting...and waiting.

It was now 2:42. I give everyone at least 15 minutes leeway if I don't hear from them, and that window was about to close tighter than the lid on Dracula's coffin. I was just about to give up when I saw her walking toward me. My heart rate kicked up a notch as we said

Hi.

Déjà vu all over again! This was starting to sound like our IM's. Anyway, we headed over to the bar for a drink. The Initial Interview went extremely well, ending up with a very nice prolonged goodbye kiss behind the escalator near the baggage claim area. To make a long story short, my bride and I are living proof that Internet Dating works. Our story has a very happy ending, and I hope yours does too!

Now that I am married I am finding out once again that the male species never gets the final word so, here is...

Marcia's Side of the Story

Truth be known, I saw Jon's profile and the fact that he was moving south to Fort Lauderdale, and I thought long and hard about sending him an email. He mentioned that he didn't like long-distance relationships, and I was not looking to really date anyone out of the Miami area. But I thought he looked nice and his profile was appealing, so I sent an email. In retrospect, what I wrote was really corny, and when he didn't respond, I figured he wasn't interested or he thought I was an idiot. To hear him tell it, he had so many emails (by the way, I believe the men on Internet Dating sites receive more emails than women) that he hadn't gotten around to responding yet. But again, with persistence and a few IM's, a phone call, and the first meeting, the rest is history.

Jon and Marcia on a recent cruise
through the Panama Canal

Appendix: Chat Lingo

For your convenience, here's a handy list of commonly used Chat Room Lingo and a few of the acronyms used in the book:

AIM: AOL Instant Messenger
AFAIK: As Far As I Know
AFK: Away From Keyboard
AMIIC: Ask Me If I Care
AOL: America Online
ASAP: As Soon As Possible
A/S/L: Age, Sex, and Location

BAS: Big Ass Smile
BBL: Be Back Later
BBN: Bye Bye Now
BBS: Be Back Soon
BEG: Big Evil Grin
BF: Boyfriend
BIBO: Beer In, Beer Out
BRB: Be Right Back
BTW: By The Way
BWL: Bursting With Laughter

C&G: Chuckle and Grin
CICO: Coffee In, Coffee Out
CID: Crying In Disgrace
CRBT: Crying Real Big Tears
CSG: Chuckle Snicker Grin
CYA: See Ya

CYAL8R: See You Later

DBAS: Don't Be A Stranger
DLTBBB: Don't Let The Bed Bugs Bite

EG: Evil Grin

FC: Fingers Crossed
FTBOMH: From the Bottom of My Heart
FYI: For Your Information
FWIW: For What It's Worth

G: Grin
GA: Go Ahead
GAL: Get A Life
GF: Girlfriend
GFN: Gone For Now
GMBO: Giggling My Butt Off
GMTA: Great Minds Think Alike
GTSY: Glad To See You

H: Hug
H&K: Hug and Kiss
HABU: Have A Better 'Un
HAGN: Have A Good Night
HAGU: Have A Good 'Un
HAHA: Having A Heart Attack
HHH: Har Har Har
HHIS: Hanging Head in Shame
HUB: Head Up Butt

IAE: In Any Event
IC: I See
ICQ: Internet Chat/Instant Messenger
IGP: I Gotta Pee
IMNSHO: In My Not So Humble Opinion

IMO: In My Opinion
IMCO: In My Considered Opinion
IMHO: In My Humble Opinion
IOW: In Other Words
IRL: In Real Life
ITA: I Totally Agree
IWALU: I Will Always Love You

JJ: Just Joking
JK: Just Kidding
JMO: Just My Opinion
JTLYK: Just To Let You Know

K: Kiss
KIT: Keep In Touch
KOC: Kiss On Cheek
KOL: Kiss On Lips
KWIM: Know What I mean

L: Laugh
L8R: Later
L8RG8R: Later Gator
LHM: Lord Help Me
LHO: Laughing Head Off
LHU: Lord Help Us
LMAO: Laughing My Ass Off
LMCAO: Laughing My Cute Ass Off
LMFAO: Laughing My F***ing Ass Off
LMSO: Laughing My Socks Off
LOL: Laugh Out Loud
LTNS: Long Time No See
LTS: Laughing To Self
LUWAMH: Love You With All My Heart
LY: Love You

MTF: More To Follow
MYOB: Mind Your Own Business

MUI: Meeting Under the Influence

NP: No Problem
NRN: No Reply Necessary

OIC: Oh, I See
OL: Old Lady (significant other)
OM: Old Man (significant other)
OTOH: On The Other Hand
OTTOMH: Off The Top of My Head

PITA: Pain In The Ass
PM: Private Message
PMFJI: Pardon Me For Jumping In
PIMP: Peed In My Pants
POAHF: Put On A Happy Face
POV: Point Of View
PPL: People

QSL: Reply
QSO: Conversation
QT: Cutie

ROFL: Rolling On Floor Laughing
ROFLAPMP: ROFL And Peeing My Pants
ROFLMAO: ROFL My Ass Off
RSN: Real Soon Now
RTFM: Read The F***ing Manual!

S: Smile
SETE: Smiling Ear To Ear
Snail Mail: U.S. Mail System
SNERT: Snot-Nosed Egotistical Rude Teenager
SO: Significant Other
SOT: Short Of Time
SOTMG: Short Of Time Must Go

SWAK: Sealed With A Kiss
SWAG: Scientific Wild Ass Guess
SWL: Screaming with Laughter
SYS: See You Soon

TA: Thanks Again
TG: Thank God
TGIF: Thank God It's Friday
TCOY: Take Care Of Yourself
TILII: Tell It Like It Is
TMI: Too Much Information
TMFI: Too Much F***ing Information
TNT: Till Next Time
TOY: Thinking Of You
TTC: Trying To Conceive
TTFN: Ta Ta For Now
TTYL: Talk To You Later
TY: Thank You

W: Wink
WAG: Wild Ass Guess
WB: Welcome Back
WTG: Way To Go

YBS: You'll Be Sorry
YG: Young Gentleman
YL: Young Lady
YM: Young Man
YW: You're Welcome

About the Author

Jon Rubin grew up (assuming that he grew up at all) in Deerfield and Highland Park, Illinois, just north of Chicago. He enjoyed swimming, football, baseball, pole vaulting and chasing members of the opposite sex as fun ways to endure his formative years. He was certified as a SCUBA Diver at the age of 14, and at the age of 16 he was one of, if not the youngest, individuals at the time to host a commercial radio talk show.

The show was called "Speak Out," and aired in Chicago on WEEF AM & FM. At the age of 21, he earned his pilot's license, and opened a restaurant, which he sold several years later when he decided to pursue a successful career in the computer software industry. Mr. Rubin founded his second company, a software development and consulting group, in 1987, and went out on his own in 1991.

In 1992, he decided that he never wanted to be on his death bed saying, "I would of...I could of...I should of," so he threw his hat into the political arena and, though unsuccessful, he ran for the state legislature. Along the way, he created and produced several television shows, the most recent being "Skating's Next Star" hosted by Kristi Yamaguchi, and is currently working on several other productions.

Jon was found for the final time on an Internet Dating site by Marcia. They were married in 2005, and they live together in bliss and happiness in South Florida. When asked why they married after only 13 months of dating, Marcia points out that since they are in their early 50's, each year that passes is like a dog year. So in a weird sort of way, they dated for over 7 years before the wedding. Together, they have four wonderful adult children.

You can find them at the theater, a restaurant or out at a night club listening and dancing to the music of the '60s and '70s. They can also be found several times a year on a cruise ship somewhere in the world.

Notes

Notes

Notes

Printed in the United States
200104BV00002B/556-690/A

9 780979 514425